FAN PHENOMENA

# THE BIG LEBOWSKI

EDITED BY
ZACHARY INGLE

# Credits

First Published in the UK in 2014 by Intellect Books, The Mill, Parnall Road, Fishponds, Bristol, BS16 3JG, UK

First Published in the USA in 2014 by Intellect Books, The University of Chicago Press, 1427 E. 60th Street, Chicago, IL 60637, USA



Editor: Zachary Ingle

Series Editor and Design: Gabriel Solomons

Typesetting: Stephanie Sarlos

Copy Editor: Emma Rhys



A Catalogue record for this book is available from the British Library

**Fan Phenomena Series**
ISSN: 2051-4468
eISSN: 2051-4476

**Fan Phenomena: The Big Lebowski**
ISBN: 978-1-78320-202-7
eISBN: 978-1-78320-247-8 / 978-1-78320-246-1

intellect

# Contents

# Acknowledgements


**Acknowledgments**

*Fan Phenomena: The Big Lebowski* would not have been possible without my compeers in this enterprise, the contributors to this volume, who achieved the modest task that was their charge. One might expect Lebowski fans to be a little more Dude-like and not even know what day of the week it is, much less be able to pay attention to deadlines, but that was not the case with this diligent bunch of Achievers.

I would also like to thank Intellect for its dogged pursuit toward publishing books that fill voids in film scholarship, while also being accessible for the general reader. I have been an avid reader (and collector) of Intellect's film books since the first entry in the Directory of World Cinema series (Japan, edited by John Berra). After writing for several books published by Intellect, it is an honour to have this opportunity to edit my own. There are several individuals I would like to thank: Kim Barber, Adam Bertocci and Will Russell, for their willingness to be interviewed for this volume; Jeremy Hehl, who was a tremendous help during the latter stages of this book; Marcelline Block and John Berra, editors of several books for Intellect, both of whom I now consider friends, and who have modelled for me what it means to be a good editor; Mika Elovaara, also inspirational with his excellent work editing *Fan Phenomena: Star Wars*; series editor Gabriel Solomons, a pleasure to work with, patient with me and reminding me of the necessity of deadlines; and Robert Reed, who tried to convince me of *The Big Lebowski*'s greatness before I finally 'saw the light'. I would especially like to thank my accommodating wife, Jemima, who puts up with all of my 'crazy projects'.

**Zachary Ingle, Editor**

# Introduction
# Zachary Ingle

→ **How did *The Big Lebowski* (Joel and Ethan Coen, 1998) became the most significant cult film of the last thirty years? Since the film's release, can you name another movie that has inspired several conventions for its fans (who are affectionately known as 'Achievers') held throughout the world every year? Do any other American films from 1998 seem nearly as important in hindsight as *The Big Lebowski*, including those that grossed several times over *Lebowski*'s disappointing $46 million worldwide take? (I'm looking at you *Armageddon* [Michael Bay, $553 million], *Godzilla* [Roland Emmerich, $379 million] and *Doctor Dolittle* [Betty Thomas, $294 million].) Yet by 2010, it headed *Total Film*'s list of 'The 34 Greatest Cult Films of All Time' and now makes frequent appearances on 'greatest films' lists.**

Like many of you, I did not see *The Big Lebowski* in its original theatrical run. When I first saw the film (probably on the Comedy Channel with its infamous bowdlerizations such as 'This is what happens when you find a stranger in the Alps!'), I thought it was a good film, but rather average for the Coen brothers. But whether it is *Fargo* (1996) or *Intolerable Cruelty* (2003), their films are enriched with repeated viewings, perhaps more so than any other film-makers. As I saw it a second and a third time, the brilliance of its dialogue stuck with me, and when I decided to write about the film for one of my first papers as a graduate student (comparing the misconceptions of nihilism in both it and Fyodor Dostoevsky's *Demons* [1872] – okay, so there wasn't a *literal connection*), I was hooked, finally understanding what all the hubbub was about. (White Russians would forever afterward also be this former teetotaler's drink of choice.) Why do I identify with The Dude? I have never smoked pot, haven't dropped an F-bomb since the third grade, my attitude towards Los Angeles has been influenced too much by Alvy Singer's (Woody Allen) insults of the city in *Annie Hall* (Woody Allen, 1977), and am too much of a workaholic (occupying the classroom rather than various administration buildings) to identify with the Dude's easy-going personality. And yet, I still feel like a kindred spirit with the Dude. The film resonates with me, and since you are reading this book, I would guess it probably does with you as well.

This volume on *The Big Lebowski* is a unique entry in the Fan Phenomena series. Others are based on a series, whether book (*The Hunger Games*) or television (*Twin Peaks, Doctor Who, Buffy the Vampire Slayer, Supernatural*), individuals (*Audrey Hepburn, Marilyn Monroe*), or transmedia cultural behemoths (*Star Trek, Star Wars, Batman, Sherlock Holmes*). With the possible exception of *Twin Peaks*, *The Big Lebowski* further stands out within the Fan Phenomena series in that it is the only volume so far that is not classified as a generic (sci-fi/fantasy/superhero) text or based on the cult of a star. Certainly *The Big Lebowski* has generic elements, including Chandleresque mystery, Berkeleyesque musical, and western traits, but it cannot be easily identified by genre nor is it the type of text like *Star Wars*, *Star Trek* or *Doctor Who* that packs in legions of devotees at comic conventions. Additionally, *The Big Lebowski* singles itself out as the most 'contained' text. *Star Trek* and *Star Wars* have spawned numerous films, television series, novels, comic books, etc., and *Doctor Who* is on its Twelfth Doctor, while *The Big Lebowski* has no sequels, remakes or adaptations. Fan activity largely centres on festivals and cosplay, rather than phenomena like fanfiction, video games or collecting action figures. In other words, the fan phenomena of *The Big Lebowski* is based on a two-hour experience (albeit one repeated multiple times). It is a testament to the fervent fan following of the film that it would even deserve to be one of the first volumes in this series.

In this, the first academic book devoted entirely to Lebowski fandom, ten aca-fans

**Introduction**
Zachary Ingle

(Henry Jenkins's designation for those scholars who have emerged out of the fan community) have penned chapters devoted to various aspects of the Lebowski cultus, offering a variety of approaches. Fans often cite the film's dialogue as the most enthralling aspect of the film; Jeff Jaeckle examines the role of repetition in 'The Comforts and Pleasures of Repetitive Dialogue in *The Big Lebowski*'. Randall Clark's 'Another Caucasian: Online Fan Response to Donny and the Stranger' tracks online fandom, including Lebowski websites, Facebook pages, and YouTube videos, but focuses on the attention garnered for even peripheral characters like Donny and the Stranger. Jeremy Hehl's chapter, '"If You Will It, It Is No Dream": Lebowski Fest and Cult Fandom', offers a glimpse at Lebowski Fest, perhaps *the* most distinctive aspect about Lebowski fandom. While *The Big Lebowski* has not spawned the ancillary merchandise of a *Star Wars* or *The Lord of the Rings*, there are several collectible artefacts out there for the diehard Achiever, as catalogued in Andrew Howe's chapter 'That Shirt Really Ties the Room Together: The Lebowski Legacy of Cultural Artefacts'. That *The Big Lebowski* has become one of the most prominent cult films in history is without question; Keith Clavin compares this cult fandom of it to other films of its time (*Fight Club* [David Fincher, 1999] and *Fear and Loathing in Las Vegas* [Terry Gilliam, 1998], among others) and how they attempted to redefine masculinity in his chapter, 'Nihilistic Dudes: The Masculine Cult Figure in *Fin de Siècle* American Cinema'. Paul Rogalus's 'The Bard, The Knave and Sir Walter: Adapting a Modern Cult Movie into a Neo-Shakespearean Stage Play' closely scrutinizes a major Lebowski fanwork, Adam Bertocci's play *Two Gentlemen of Lebowski* (2010). In her chapter 'Reimagining and Commodifying Gender, Genre and Sexuality in *The Big Lebowski* for Cult Fan Consumption', Sheri Chinen Biesen first dissects the various generic tropes of the film and its effects on fandom before examining how Lebowski fandom is coded along gender and sexual lines. Peter C. Kunze 'show[s] how the rise of the Internet, somewhat paralleled to *The Big Lebowski*'s own rise, has allowed for extensions on existing fan practices and the rapid development of new fields of interactions between viewers' in 'The Dude Goes Digital: *The Big Lebowski*, New Media and Participatory Culture'. In 'Listening Deeply to *Lebowski:* One Fan's Attempt to Draw a Musical Map Surrounding the Dude' Tom Zlabinger charts how music works in the film, as well as how it affects fan reaction. Considering that *The Big Lebowski* has spawned its own religion, Dudeism, with its ordained priests and 'sacred' texts (*The Dude De Ching* [2010]), the religio-philosophical response of fans to the film was essential to scrutinize; JZ Long notes how fans have traced the origins of Dudeism in Daoism and Buddhism in his chapter 'Abiding Sublimely: From Eastern Philosophies to *The Big Lebowski*'.

Included herein are also three interviews with major figures associated with Lebowski fandom. Will Russell, co-founder of Lebowski Fest and co-author of *I'm a Lebowski, You're a Lebowski: Life, The Big Lebowski, and What Have You* (2007), has established himself as one of the most prominent voices in Achiever culture. The second interview is with Adam Bertocci, author of *Two Gentlemen of Lebowski*, a Shakespearean take on

the film. Finally, Kim Barber shares her experience working on *The Achievers* (2009), a documentary on *Lebowski* fandom. All three interviewees offer their insight into how fandom can be a creative process in its own right, and not simply a passive enterprise.
In keeping with the Fan Phenomena series, chapters are written for scholars, fans and aca-fans alike. Sure there are other books out there about *The Big Lebowski* (and I'm pretty sure I've read them all), which suggests the depths of the film and the pleasures we gain from reading about it. But just as the film is worth watching over and over, there is room for one more book. I guess that's the way the whole durned human comedy keeps perpetuatin' itself. ●

Chapter

1

# The Comforts and Pleasures of Repetitive Dialogue in *The Big Lebowski*

Jeff Jaeckle

→ ***The Big Lebowski* can be a difficult film, especially for first-time audiences. While not as cerebral as *Barton Fink* (1991), nor as graphically violent as *Miller's Crossing* (1990) and *Fargo* (1996), the film's sprawling plot and barrage of cultural references are nonetheless tricky. As the eclectic cast of over three dozen characters wanders through Los Angeles, bizarre storylines intersect, often resulting in narrative detours and dead ends, including kidnapping, embezzlement, the adult film industry, community theatre, castration, pregnancy and, of course, a bowling tournament.**

Peppered throughout are allusions to popular and high culture, which the characters use with little context, among them nihilism, the Biennale, National Socialism, Theodor Herzl, the first Gulf War, Vladimir Lenin and human paraquats.

Unsurprisingly, many early reviews were negative, with critics claiming that the film's plotting and allusions made it 'deliriously fractured' (*The Hollywood Reporter*), 'incomprehensible' (*Time*), 'hopelessly twisted up' (*New Statesman*) and 'thick with non-sequiturs' (*Sight and Sound*), thus ensuring 'an almost complete lack of structural integrity' (*Boxoffice*). These reviews make the film sound onerous and pretentious, yet *The Big Lebowski* is perhaps the most popular cult film of the early twenty-first century. The preponderance of midnight screenings and festivals, special editions and merchandizing, and numerous books on its making, philosophy, religious significance and all-around brilliance suggest that the film's difficulty is not overwhelming, nor without its admirers.

One possibility is that fans enjoy the film *despite* its difficulty. They can delight in its surreal dream sequences and bawdy humour without becoming bothered by, for instance, Bunny Lebowski's (Tara Reid) unexplained motivations for leaving Minnesota or the vague logic of the Dude's (Jeff Bridges) insult of the Big Lebowski (David Huddleston) as a 'human paraquat' – an oblique reference to a herbicide once used by the US government to destroy marijuana plantations. This pick-and-choose experience could effectively pare the film down to a simple buddy flick or, as film critic David Edelstein puts it, a 'scattershot druggy' comedy in the tradition of the Cheech and Chong series (Tommy Chong and Cheech Marin, 1978–84). Another possibility is that fans appreciate the film *because* of its difficulty, giving over to and relishing in its sheer complexity. *Sight and Sound* critic Jonathan Romney suggests that, for these types of fans, the 'story enables us to enjoy a whole catalogue of narrative dead ends, cruel gags and bravura character routines'. Repeat viewings would only strengthen these pleasures, as audiences could easily rekindle their stoner experiences or diligently seek out new details and references.

But what about first-time audiences faced with confusing plots and obscure allusions? How do they navigate these twists and turns, and what keeps them in their seats for the duration of the nearly two-hour film? To paraphrase the Dude, what ties the movie together? One possibility is *mise-en-scène*. Given that the entire film is set in and around Los Angeles, audiences can conceivably latch on to geography to ground their experiences of the film. However, the visual palates of these locations – like Los Angeles itself – vary widely. In *The Big Lebowski: The Making of a Coen Brothers Film* (1998), cinematographer Roger Deakins admits, 'I'm not sure I ever really had a handle on what *Lebowski* should look like [...] It's such a mix, I don't think it has one style.' In an interview for the same book, Joel Coen concurs, 'There are parts of the movie that want to be

**The Comforts and Pleasures of Repetitive Dialogue in *The Big Lebowski***
Jeff Jaeckle

*Fig. 1 - 3: Examples of visual discontinuity in* The Big Lebowski

real and contemporary-feeling and other things that are very stylized, like the dream sequences. And then there's the bowling stuff. So this is more of a mix.'

As these shots of the bowling alley, the Dude's drug-induced dream and Larry Sellers' house illustrate, the compositions of these scenes are quite distinct, hardly making *mise-en-scène* a through-line for audiences.

Another unifying feature could be the Dude, who appears on-screen in all of these visually disparate settings and interacts with every character. However, the Dude isn't the most articulate of guides. He frequently finds himself overwhelmed, admitting at one point to Maude Lebowski (Julianne Moore), 'There are a lotta ins, a lotta outs, a lotta what-have-yous. And, uh, a lotta strands to keep in my head, man.' When he attempts to explain his experiences, the Dude is often unreliable, uttering ill-formed or nonsensical lines. According to Paul Coughlin, in his essay for the *Film Journal*, the entire movie is based on such nonsense, 'embodied in the Dude's inability to verbalize anything remotely like a reasonable explanation for his circumstances'. The same could be said of the film's other potential guide, the Stranger (Sam Elliott), a voice-over narrator that loses his train of thought in the film's opening scene.

So, then, if the linchpin of *The Big Lebowski* is not any single plot, location or character, what holds it together? I propose that the answers are found in the film's sound design, specifically its uses of dialogue. As James Mottram explains in *Coen Brothers: The Life of the Mind* (2000), 'Wayward as the script may be [...] what distinguishes the film from any [other], again, is the attention paid to speech patterns.' He is especially struck by the repetitive nature of these patterns, which 'flood the film, with characters reusing each others' words sub-consciously'. Justus Nieland dubs these patterns 'Dudespeak', in *The Year's Work in Lebowski Studies* (2009), arguing for the importance of mimicry, 'a compulsive borrowing from the stylized tissue of verbiage whose repetitions, loopings and displacements constitute the film's linguistic world'. For first-time audiences, these repetitions lend coherence to the film's sprawling plot and perplexing allusions, making it more comprehensible. For repeat audiences, they reward close listening by making the film into an aural game based on short-term memory skills and adept recollection. In short, these dialogue patterns draw us into the film and keep us coming back for more.

In these respects, *The Big Lebowski* meets a chief criterion of cult films, as defined by Umberto Eco in his oft-cited essay, '*Casablanca*: Cult Movies and Intertextual Collage' (1985): 'It must provide a completely furnished world, so that its fans can quote characters and episodes as if they were part of the beliefs of a sect, a private world of their own, a world about which one can play puzzle games and trivia contests.' *The Big Lebowski* is satisfying as a cult film, in part, because it provides first-time and repeat audiences a world of eminently quotable lines that aid comprehension and encourage verbal gamesmanship. Regardless of what happens, who appears on-screen or what characters allude to, the film's dialogue keeps audiences comfortably on track while

**The Comforts and Pleasures of Repetitive Dialogue in *The Big Lebowski***
Jeff Jaeckle

providing aesthetic pleasures based on repetition.

## Verbal coherence

Recounting the plot of *The Big Lebowski* is akin to telling a riddle. Why would a draft-dodging stoner and a militant Vietnam veteran be best friends? What do an unemployed bowler and a wheelchair-bound philanthropist have in common? What connects muscle-bound, porn-star thugs to skinny, leather-glad nihilists? Even when using character names, these questions can be difficult to answer, especially when removing the superficial response of 'the Dude'. What connects Maude and Walter Sobchack (John Goodman)? What do Larry Sellers (Jesse Flanagan) and Uli Kunkel (Peter Stormare) have in common? What links Walter with the Malibu Chief of Police (Leon Russom)? The answer is dialogue, as characters that would otherwise have no relationship find themselves drawn together through language. The Coens' strategies here are twofold: repetitive dialogue simplifies characterization, making the large cast easier to distinguish and recall, while dialogue echoes link seemingly unrelated locations, characters and events.

The Coens exaggerate verbal repetition to the level of parody in *The Big Lebowski*, often reducing characters to easily graspable types; their repeated phrases become shorthand descriptors - a form of verbal typecasting - much like product slogans. For instance, the band of German Nihilists that claim to have kidnapped Bunny and threaten to castrate the Dude are quickly summed up in the phrase 'funny stuff', which appears in the text of their ransom note, during the ransom drop off, in their initial attack on the Dude and in their final encounter with him, Walter and Donny (Steve Buscemi) - a total of six times. The repeated line betrays their amateur status and marks them, ironically, as 'funny' characters: comically inexperienced and inept kidnappers. As J. M. Tyree and Ben Walters note in their BFI guide to the film, 'by the fifth time the nihilists warn against the consequences of "funny stuff", it's clear there's nothing to worry about'. Instead of needing to recognize and distinguish these three characters, audiences can recall one simple and silly idea whenever they appear on-screen. Likewise, the Big Lebowski's use of 'bums', which he applies on nine occasions to the Dude and any man who fails to achieve his professional goals, reduces the character to a rabid classist; this repetition also typecasts him as an aggressive and economically powerful antagonist to our mellow and unemployed protagonist, the Dude. (Seasoned audiences also recognize 'bum' as a Freudian slip that reveals the Big Lebowski's anxieties about subsisting entirely on his deceased wife's inheritance).

Perhaps the most condensed form of verbal typecasting occurs when the Dude is brought before the Malibu Chief of Police, a fascistic disciplinarian who recalls the character of Gunnery Sergeant Hartman (R. Lee Ermey) in Stanley Kubrick's *Full Metal Jacket* (1987). In under two minutes, the character's repetitive dialogue makes plain his function in the film in relation to the Dude: 'I don't like your jerkoff name. I don't like your jerkoff face. I don't like your jerkoff behavior. And I don't like you, jerkoff.' As with the Nihilists' repetition of 'funny stuff', the police chief's use of 'jerkoff' stands in for the character: he's the kind of jerkoff against which the Dude defines himself, making him another obvious antagonist. Audiences don't need to think much more about him.

When shared between multiple characters, repetitive dialogue links disparate events and locations. In some cases, characters recycle lines they overhear, which recalls and clarifies aspects of one scene in another. The ransom plot, for instance, is held together in part by a grave proclamation about the kidnapped Bunny. The Big Lebowski's assistant Brandt (Philip Seymour Hoffman) initiates the pattern when stressing that the Dude is in a position to save Bunny by delivering the ransom: 'Her life is in your hands' – a line that his employer asks him to repeat. Later that evening, minutes before the Dude and Walter botch their mission, the Dude laments, 'Her life was in our hands!' Days later, when the Dude meets again with the Big Lebowski, the enraged husband insists, 'Her *life* was in your *hands*!' These repetitions make the apparent purpose of these characters' actions impossible to mistake; despite the chaos and confusion surrounding the kidnapping and ransom, this line makes the plot fairly obvious, if not overly simplistic. (For seasoned audiences, the line also masks the truth that Bunny's life is in her *own* hands, since she never was kidnapped.)

The Coens take repetitive dialogue even further by creating lines that pass between characters that do not share the screen. Nieland refers to these as '*impossible* repetitions' in which 'characters recycle fragments of speech from contexts in which they were not physically present as auditors' (original emphasis). Although these repetitions are admittedly subtle and fleeting, they nonetheless connect these characters and provide some measure of coherence. Take the terms 'jerkoff' and 'goldbricker', two unusual words that become more conspicuous because of their frequent repetition. The Dude starts the pattern when telling adult-film mogul Jackie Treehorn (Ben Gazzara), 'Yeah, well, I still jerkoff manually,' in response to his account of the frontiers of electronic porn. After Treehorn drugs the Dude and throws him on the streets of Malibu, the Dude encounters the chief of police, who repeats 'jerkoff' four times (see above); he also introduces the term 'goldbricker' when demanding, 'Keep your ugly, fucking goldbricking ass out of my beach community.' Later that night, when the Dude solves the mystery of the missing ransom, Walter uses the term to castigate the Big Lebowski for embezzling funds from the Achiever's Foundation and for pretending (he believes) to be paraplegic: 'This guy's a fake. A fucking goldbricker.' These repetitions verbally link these characters and scenes while drawing parallels between ostensibly opposed situations, such as the ways in which the two Jeffrey Lebowskis are, as the police chief and Walter insist, goldbrickers. The same can be said of other shared terms, among them 'clams' (Maude and Walter), 'amateurs' (Jackie Treehorn and Walter) and 'johnson' (Maude, the Dude, and the Nihilists) – these words connect characters through language while encouraging audiences to consider deeper similarities.

Verbal typecasting and echoes make *The Big Lebowski* more coherent and comprehensible; however, these dialogue patterns don't always do the trick. Some first-time viewers still find the film unfathomable. For these audiences, the only solution is to rewatch the movie, so that the incantatory power of its dialogue can take root. Anecdotes of these viewing experiences abound online, such as this one from a fan in Poland, which Barbara Klinger records in her article on *The Big Lebowski* for the journal *Screen*: 'The film really didn't seem interesting after the first viewing, but when I saw it a second, third time (via repeats on cable TV), everything changed. I [found] brilliant dialogue [...] favorite lines, hidden comic situations that one must really see the film a few times to notice.' These fans go beyond mere comprehension of the film to relish in dialogue complexities that reward close listening and encourage verbal gamesmanship.

## Word games

Among diehard fans of *The Big Lebowski*, a badge of honour is the ability to recall and recite the film's dialogue flawlessly. As editors Aaron Jaffe and Edward P. Comentale explain in their introduction to *The Year's Work in Lebowski Studies*, 'there are essentially two behaviors central to the cult: catchphrases and dressing up. We'd argue that both have less to do with identification than achievements in citation'. Referring to the game-like aspects of this dialogue, they observe that diehard fans 'refuse to limit themselves to the Coens' most pithy utterances, but retrieve lines wholesale from the multiple viewings as if pulling pieces from a large puzzle box'. *The Big Lebowski* offers these verbal puzzle pieces in droves, rewarding audience members who listen closely and frequently.

The simplest reward is the pleasure of reciting the dialogue, which fans often do by yelling the movie's many quotable lines at the screen. Film blogger Julian Ayrs explains, many fans seem to have 'caught an infectious bug [...] that compels them to return to each screening [and] scream out dialogue amid a raucous round of wild guffaws'. Perhaps the quintessential example of this scream-worthy dialogue comes during Walter's destruction of a new corvette, during which he exclaims, 'This is what happens when you fuck a stranger in the ass!' The seventeen variations of this line make it highly quotable, while an exact recitation of Walter's monologue would likely constitute what Jaffe and Comentale describe as an 'achievement in citation'. Much is true of other catchphrases, including 'shut the fuck up [Donny]' (7×), 'is this your homework?' (5×), 'where's the [fucking] money?' (5×) and 'a world of pain' (4×). Each example attests to what Klinger dubs 'replay culture' in which, through repeat screenings, 'dialogue may be burned into the viewer's memory, becoming signature aspects of meaning and pleasure'. *The Big Lebowski* taps into this culture by building replay into the film itself: the repetitive nature of the dialogue makes it more memorable and pleasurable to recall.

Perhaps the chief source of replay pleasure is the film's litany of curse words. Recognizing every variation of the word 'fuck', for instance, is no small feat; it is also a celebrated one, as Jenny M. Jones makes clear in her illustrated and annotated history of *The Big Lebowski* when referring to the 'gloriously profane montage of "fuck", fucks", "fucked", "fucking", fuckin'" and one "camelfucker"'. Yet this preponderance is dwarfed when adding in all of the film's curse words. Tyree and Walters provide this overview: 'the movie uses the word "fuck" and its derivatives more than 260 times – on average, once every twenty-five seconds – along with other profanities including, but not limited to, thirty-seven shits, six assholes, two bitches and a bastard.' Unsurprisingly, some fans have showcased their knowledge of these repetitions by cataloguing every one of them in YouTube videos, including 'The Big Lebowski: The Fucking Short Version' and 'Big Lebowski: Every Single God Damned Shit Fucking Swear'. In daily contexts, the ability to recall and recite these strings of curse words can serve as both personal delight and social achievement.

Finally, one of the most sophisticated forms of replay pleasure in *The Big Lebowski* comes in appreciating the numerous terms for concepts that, to draw on another repeated phrase, are uttered in 'the parlance of our times'. Given the characters' preoccupations with sex, these terms tend to be erotic in nature. Jones catalogs a number of these, including variations on male genitalia (cock, a pair of testicles, dick, rod, johnson and viggly penis) and X-rated cinema (pornography, beaver picture, smut business and adult entertainment). The game here is for audiences to recognize the pattern and track its variations – yet another task that rewards attentiveness to dialogue, especially verbal nuance. Collectively, these repetitive words and phrases make for a more interactive filmgoing experience, inviting audiences to study the movie, share their knowledge and reap the honours and joys of achievement.

### Conclusion

Repetitive dialogue in *The Big Lebowski* lends coherence to the film's disjointed plot and obscure allusions while inviting audiences to participate in word games that reward close listening. These dialogue patterns, although certainly pronounced in *The Big Lebowski*, are indicative of every Coen film. For instance, the Nihilists' emphasis on avoiding 'funny stuff' is not unlike numerous characters' descriptions of Carl Showalter (Steve Buscemi) as 'funny looking' in *Fargo*, nor is it dissimilar from the characters' expressed doubts that Abby (Frances McDormand) 'ain't done nothing funny' in *Blood Simple* (1984). A smattering of catchphrases from other films shows that a frequent and successful strategy for the Coens is to construct dialogue that taps into these pleasures of repetition: 'Say, that reminds me' (*Raising Arizona* [1987]), 'What's the rumpus?' (*Miller's Crossing*), 'You know, for kids' (*The Hudsucker Proxy* [1994]) and 'Damn, we're in a tight spot' (*O Brother, Where Art Thou?* [2000]).

These are just some of the dozens of lines that showcase the Coens' talents for crafting cult film dialogue. The film-makers have a knack for cultivating an audience's self-conscious relationship with language, encouraging us to recognize repeated phrases, appreciate their density and complexity, memorize them and incorporate them into our daily speech. In this way, the Coens might be considered cult auteurs, with *The Big Lebowski* standing as their greatest cult achievement so far. ●

## GO FURTHER

### Books

*The Big Lebowski: An Illustrated, Annotated History of the Greatest Cult Film of All Time*
Jenny M. Jones
(Minneapolis: Voyageur, 2012)

*The Year's Work in Lebowski Studies*
Edward P. Comentale and Aaron Jaffe (eds)
(Bloomington: Indiana University Press, 2009)

*The Big Lebowski* (BFI Film Classics)
J. M. Tyree and Ben Walters
(London: BFI, 2007)

*Coen Brothers: The Life of the Mind*
James Mottram
(Dulles: Brassey's, 2000)

*The Big Lebowski: The Making of a Coen Brothers Film*
Tricia Cooke and William Preston Robertson (eds.)
(New York: W. W. Norton, 1998)

### Extracts/Essays/Articles

'Becoming Cult: *The Big Lebowski*, Replay Culture and Male Fans'
Barbara Klinger
In *Screen*. 51: 1 (2010), pp. 1–20.

'You're Entering a World of Lebowski'
David Edelstein
In *New York Times*, 8 August 2004, Available at: http://www.nytimes.com

'*Casablanca*: Cult Movies and Intertextual Collage'
Umberto Eco
In *Substance*. 14: 2 (1985), pp. 3–12.

**Online**

'*The Big Lebowski*: The Fucking Short Version' [YouTube], 18 July 2006, www.youtube.com/watch?v=gU2ZgaQ_H-Y.

'*Big Lebowski*: Every Single God Damned Shit Fucking Swear' [YouTube], 16 September 2007,
www.youtube.com/watch?v=xf7frtuyF14.

'*The Big Lebowski* ... fans storm theatre'
Julian Ayrs
*The Tattler*. 5 November 2007, www.ijulian.blogspot.com/2007/11/big-lebowski-fan-storm-theatre-time-for.html.

'Language Aesthetics in Three Films by Joel and Ethan Coen'
Paul Coughlin
*The Film Journal*. No. 12, www.thefilmjournal.com.

Chapter 2

# Another Caucasian: Online Fan Response to Donny and the Stranger

Randall Clark

→ **Actor Steve Buscemi has had a varied career. He's starred in *Boardwalk Empire* (Terence Winter, HBO, 2010- ) for Martin Scorsese; played Mr Pink in Quentin Tarantino's *Reservoir Dogs* (1992); appeared in big-budget Jerry Bruckheimer escapism like *Con Air* (Simon West, 1997) and *Armageddon* (Michael Bay, 1998); provided the voice of a monster in *Monsters, Inc.* (Pixar, 2001); had recurring roles on both *The Sopranos* (HBO, 1999-2007) and *30 Rock* (Tina Fey, NBC, 2006-2013); and even played one of the two title characters in *Ed and His Dead Mother* (Jonathan Wacks, 1993).**

But to a huge number of film buffs he will always be known for his work with Joel and Ethan Coen and particularly for his portrayal of Theodore Donald Kerabatsos, better known as Donny, in *The Big Lebowski*. In 2012, Buscemi was interviewed by *Rolling Stone* Magazine, with the entire interview discussing Buscemi's portrayal of Donny. In that interview, Buscemi mentions that fans of the movie have created the intriguing theory that 'Donny is just a figment of Walter's imagination. Like he's an old army buddy that had died or something', and concedes that 'It almost works'. Although that theory was almost certainly spawned during late-night conversations between Lebowski fans, it is the Internet that made that theory more than just random speculation between buddies and actually put it out before the public to be debated. The Donny theory is, in fact, part of one of the more interesting online phenomena of the Lebowski cult.

Like most cult movies, *The Big Lebowski* has a strong presence on the Internet. What is interesting is the manner in which Lebowski fandom manifests itself online, what aspects of the film fans are interested in exploring. Movie cultists come to know their films by heart, which means that every aspect becomes familiar and nothing is too trivial for discussion. In the case of *The Big Lebowski*, among the many secondary elements of the movie that come up for discussion are the supporting characters, and two of the supporting characters that have a particularly significant Internet presence are Donny and the Stranger. The 'Donny isn't real' theory is not some nutty idea just tossed onto the Internet by some frivolous soul with too much time on his hands. It is actually fairly representative of how these two characters are treated by fans online.

When examining the Donny and Stranger fan responses online, the first thing one must do is notice what is *not* present. Lebowski fans are a slightly different breed from the usual cult movie fanatic – we are not dealing with the Twilight series (2008–2012) here, or even *The Rocky Horror Picture Show* (Jim Sharman, 1975). The Lebowski fan activity online is missing much of the usual fandom material. There is very little Lebowski fanfiction, for example, so we get no fabricated stories about Donny or the Stranger, no Walter/Donny "shipping', no 'big reveals' of the Stranger's background or purpose. Lebowski fans seem more interested in paying tribute to the movie than in imagining further adventures of the Dude and his friends. This is an important distinction to make because it helps explain the interest in Donny and the Stranger; if the fans aren't going to leave the world that the Coens created, then they have to satisfy themselves by examining everything within its boundaries and some things take on new meaning and become more interesting the longer you look at them.

After many years, the characters of Donny and the Stranger still lend themselves to fan discussions for a variety of reasons: important to the film but not necessarily to the plot, the Stranger serves almost entirely as a narrator, and while Donny is present in many crucial scenes, he is more of an observer than a participant most of the time. He could even be taken for the viewer's surrogate; note Walter's line, 'So you have no frame of reference here, Donny. You're like a child who wanders into the middle of a movie and wants to know ...' Furthermore, Donny does not have much background provided in the film while the Stranger has next to none at all. It is almost impossible to resist speculating about characters when the film-makers have left so many gaps to be filled in; their very non-essentialness makes the two more interesting.

So let us begin examining the fan response to these characters on the most basic level – fan quotes. All cult movies have favourite lines that fans love to repeat but *The Big Lebowski* probably has more than most. The Internet Movie Database (IMDb) lists 164 quotations from the movie, lines or even entire conversations that have been suggested by fans. Donny is represented by what is the closest thing he has to a signature line, 'I'm throwing rocks tonight', as well as, 'I am the walrus', but by no other single quotes. He shows up frequently in conversations, some of them among the most memorable from the film (and therefore, scenes that would be quoted here whether or not Donny were in them), including the nihilist conversation, Walter's Shabbos discussion and the Dude's explanation that his rug was urinated upon. Also mentioned are his line 'Phone's ringing, Dude', and the Dude's response, 'Thank you, Donny', which has taken on some significance as fans maintain that this is the only time in the film that anyone other than Walter acknowledges Donny's presence.

Donny shows up in the quotations in other ways as well. Walter's repeated 'Shut the fuck up, Donny', is catalogued as occurring five times, plus one time during which Walter only gets out 'Shut the f–' before being interrupted. Most importantly, though, Walter's eulogy for Donny has been completely reproduced and posted as a quote. This is a moving scene, particularly given the comic nature of the film, and the one scene that Donny is actually afforded some dignity; that it shows up here in its entirety speaks well of the scene but also shows how important Walter and Donny's unusual friendship is for some fans.

The Stranger fares a bit better on IMDb's quotes page. He does, after all, get to repeat one of the film's key lines, 'The Dude abides', and even add a little to it: 'I don't know about you but I take comfort in that. It's good knowin' he's out there. The Dude. Takin' 'er easy for all us sinners. Shoosh. I sure hope he makes the finals.' Other favourite quotations from the Stranger are: 'I guess that's the way the whole durned human comedy keeps perpetuatin' itself'; 'There's just one thing, Dude, do you have to use so many cuss words?'; the Chandleresque 'Darkness warshed over the Dude – darkner'n a black steer's tookus on a moonless prairie night. There was no bottom'; 'Say, friend, you got any more of that good sarsaparilla?'; and of course, 'Sometimes you eat the bar and sometimes the bar eats you'. In addition, the Stranger's lengthy monologue from the beginning of the movie is quoted here in its entirety.

Quotations show up on other webpages as well. *Sporcle*, the website that allows users to create trivia quizzes of all sorts, has seven different quizzes that ask players either to complete lines from *The Big Lebowski* or identify the speaker. There is a quiz that challenges users to repeat Donny's eulogy, word for word, and another that does the

Fig.1 : Stranger and Donny quotes on the internet

same for the Stranger's soliloquy. These quizzes go beyond just picking out quotable dialogue from a very funny movie or even paying tribute to a cherished film. They are a kind of test: if you aren't familiar with the movie then you can't complete the quizzes, so these *Sporcle* posts, created by fans of the film, serve to separate the real fans from the casual viewers.

YouTube also allows fans to compile their favourite quotations from the movie. There are several compilations of Walter saying, 'Shut the fuck up, Donny' repeatedly, and a few fans have posted individual scenes with the Stranger as well. But *Lebowski* fans have gone way beyond just putting their favourite scenes on YouTube, making some short tribute films that can be very odd indeed. Several of these videos restage the original trailer in the style of another film, so that there are *Lebowski* trailers that resemble in some way *Shrek* (Andrew Adamson, 2001), *Star Wars* (George Lucas, 1977), *300* (Zack Snyder, 2007) and *Inception* (Christopher Nolan, 2010), plus one that recreates the trailer using characters from the television series *Doctor Who*. Since the original trailer featured Donny and the Stranger briefly, so do these new versions. Donny also shows up in a brief film that adds visual effects from another Jeff Bridges movie, *Tron* (Steven Lisberger, 1982) to a scene from *The Big Lebowski* and a parody that replaces *Lebowski* characters with superheroes, with Donny playing Aquaman to the Dude's Flash, Walter's Superman and Jesus's Batman.

Some fans have recut the original trailer to make it look like a different movie; there are trailers for *The Big Lebowski* as a horror movie, a science fiction epic, an action movie and a serious thriller. Donny is more likely to show up in these than the Stranger, and one of the recut trailers is particularly interesting. One of several videos posted using only the title 'Big Lebowski Trailer Recut', this presents the movie as a tear-jerker about three close friends, the Dude, Walter and Donny, and how the two survivors cope with Donny's death. Viewers are told that 'Three friends find out ... the only thing they had ... was each other'. Donny's death scene inspired one other disconcerting video, which recreates his eulogy scene, this time replacing human actors with animated bears that first appeared in a Geico commercial. Since these fan trailers don't add anything to the movie's original story or genuinely reimagine the film – they just juxtapose dialogue with unexpected characters and visuals – they seem just to be fans having fun with a movie they really like. Making these short films is showing a sign of affection for the movie, sort of like fooling around with an old friend.

*Lebowski* fans have a presence on Facebook, which is not surprising, but what may be surprising is that this presence includes pages for many of the Lebowski characters, including Donny and even the Stranger. Perhaps appropriate, giving his mysterious nature, the Stranger's Facebook page is pretty much a complete dud. It was founded in September 2010, presumably by a fan, and after nearly three years had two posts from 'the Stranger': one merely stated 'Los Angeles' and the second asked users to name their favourite Lebowski character, a question that got two responses. That page has 112 likes. Far more people have made pages using Donny's name: there are eight under 'Donny Kerabatsos', five under 'Donald Kerabatsos' and another five with the full appellation 'Theodore Donald Kerabatsos'. Some of these pages are Facebook pages for real people who are using Donny's name rather than their own and are posting their own photos and announcements on the pages; a Facebook page under a pseudonym is not an uncommon practice, nor is using for a pseudonym the name of a fictitious character with which the user identifies. But about half of the pages are tribute pages to Donny, with made-up facts ('Interests: Bowling', 'Music: I hate the fucking Eagles'). These pages are rarely updated (if ever), although they do seem to get more visitors than the Stranger's one page. The most frequently visited Donny page was founded in 2008 and had 804 likes by 2013; it posted his eulogy and by that year had fifteen likes for the eulogy alone. These pages seem to start as larks by fans who are genuinely amused by the character and then are largely left alone by their creators, who see little need to update them regularly. (If the Dude had a webpage, he'd probably do the same.)

Some fans use the Internet to engage in serious discussions of the movie. The website *Quora* allows users to pose questions on any topic for other users to answer. There are several questions about *The Big Lebowski*, and while some are more frivolous than others, one shows that some fans do look beyond the surface of the movie. The question, 'What does Sam Elliott's the Stranger represent in the Big Lebowski?' is answered with, 'He's God. Pay attention to how he enters the scene. He's also omniscient and he doesn't like profanity.' (And then there is the question of Donny's existence ...). Several different websites, some entirely devoted to the film, others not, have addressed the theory of Donny's nonexistence, that he is merely a figment of Walter's imagination, perhaps based upon a friend of Walter's or someone with whom he served in Vietnam. The arguments against the existence of Donny are fairly consistent. He is rarely acknowledged by the Dude, apart from the time that Donny tells him his phone is ringing and the Dude says, 'Thank you, Donny.' Fans have explained this away by saying that this was just a case of the Dude humoring Walter and speaking to his imaginary friend. The bowling league seems to require players compete in teams of two; if the Dude and Walter are partners, who is Donny's teammate? Walter suffers from post-traumatic stress disorder and the Dude is, to be kind about it, sometimes oblivious to what's going on around him; Walter could have and even converse with an imaginary friend without the Dude commenting on it. A few fans have even suggested that both Donny and the Stranger are imaginary, with Donny being Walter's delusion and the Stranger being the Dude's.

Rebutting the 'Donny is not real' theory, fans have put forth the following arguments. Surely someone would comment on Walter's frequent conversations with Donny if Donny were not there. If Donny does not exist and therefore does not die, whose ashes are scattered? Jesus seems to blow a kiss directly at Donny. Donny bowls a strike and the audience actually sees the pins tumble. A few fans maintain that despite the

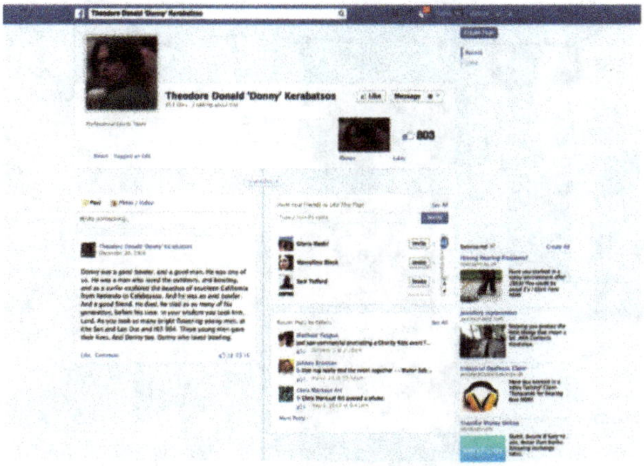

Fig. 2: Donny Facebook page

widespread idea that Donny and the Dude only interact with the 'Thank you, Donny' line, the Dude does seem to acknowledge Donny's existence in other, non-verbal ways. The theory that the Stranger is not real also does not seem to have gathered enough traction to have been debated much at all. Still, it is interesting to read the interaction of fans on these matters.

Finally, there have been webpages entirely devoted to *The Big Lebowski* that take a more academic approach to discussing the film. *Lebowskitheory.com* shut down in 2009 after publishing such pieces as 'Bowling, Gender and Emasculation in *The Big Lebowski*', but the article can still be found on the still-active site *The Dudespaper*, 'the official publication of Dudeism', which it identifies as 'the slowest growing religion in the world'. In addition to providing brief fan discussions in its forums, *The Dudespaper* regularly posts articles that analyse the film in some detail. Most of these are written by the webpage's staff, but some are submitted by fans. The Stranger and Donny show up for discussion in several of these articles, which do indeed slightly resemble scholarly works from academic publications. 'Movies That Are Rated T for Tao', for example, discusses the importance of the Stranger in the movie as he provides a philosophical note to the film. 'I Am the Walrus? Musical Representation in *The Big Lebowski*' discusses the use of music in the film as it relates to many characters, including the Stranger ('Tumbling Tumbleweeds') and Donny. A particularly interesting article, 'Unspoken Messages: Notes on Lebowskian Theory', attempts to analyse Donny and the Stranger using tarot cards. Jumping off from Walter's line to Donny – 'You are out of your element' – the article attempts to determine exactly what Donny's element is, notes that he mentions both rocks and water in the film and concludes that he is represented by the one card that encompasses both, the Star. The Stranger, whom the article points out is 'neither wholly of this time nor place' is 'firmly associated with the bush' because of the references to tumbleweeds. This article deviates a bit from the aforementioned idea that the Stranger symbolizes God by suggesting that he is in actuality an angel – 'The Stranger never walks into the view of the camera – he materializes, as it were.' A different, non-Lebowski webpage, *All Things Healing*, asserts that the Stranger is represented by the magician tarot card. The Stranger 'acts purely as an all-seeing and prescient storyteller [...] Strange things, smacking of the magical, happen when he is around'. Donny and the Stranger have moved from interesting supporting characters to symbols.

All of this web-based fan activity regarding Donny and the Stranger remains lighthearted, in keeping with the comedic spirit of the movie, even giving the appearance of casual improvisation. It allows the creators to enjoy things in life that others might see as trivial. 'The Dude abides,' the Stranger famously said. Well, thanks to the Internet, so do the Stranger and Donny. ●

*Fig. 3: illustration of a Tarot card matching the Stranger's scene*

## GO FURTHER

### Online

'Behind the Dude: Steve Buscemi on *The Big Lebowski*'
Andy Greene
Rolling Stone. 28 August 2012
www.rollingstone.com/movies/news/behind-the-dude-steve-buscemi-on-the-big-lebowski-19691231.

'*The Big Lebowski* Trailer Recut' [YouTube], 21 September 2006,
www.youtube.com/watch?v=KUJ64p3NvaA

*The Dudespaper*, dudespaper.com

'The Tarot as Frame of Reference in *The Big Lebowski*'
David Thorteinsson
*All Things Healing* (n.d.), www.allthingshealing.com.

# 'MY CALMNESS EXCEEDS THINE.'

**WALTER**
TWO GENTLEMEN OF LEBOWSKI

## Fan Appreciation no.1
## Interview with Will Russell: Co-founder of Lebowski Fest, co-author of *I'm a Lebowski, You're a Lebowski: Life, The Big Lebowski, and What Have You*

**Interview by Jeremy Hehl**

**Jeremy Hehl (JH):** *What inspired you to create the Lebowski Fest in the first place? Describe the circumstances.*

**Will Russel (WR):** We had a band, Blue Goat War, which was a terrible band and at band practice it would always end up with us trading lines of dialogue from *The Big Lebowski*. Scott [Shuffitt] and I would also vend events selling T-shirts we made and one day at a tattoo convention while bored, we were quoting lines to pass the time. Before we knew it these guys we'd never met before joined in and starting quoting lines with us. We realized we were not alone in our love of this movie, and as we watched this weird tattoo convention which culminated with people suspending from their ass piercings, inspiration struck. We thought if they can have this weird tattoo convention, we can have a *Big Lebowski* convention! I knew of a tiny bowling alley we could rent out and we printed up a few flyers and Lebowski Fest was born. We expected fifteen to twenty friends to show up but we ended up with 150 people! We decided to do it bigger the next year and due to an unexpected mention in *SPIN Magazine*'s summer events guide, had 1,200+ people show up. We took it on the road and added bands starting with My Morning Jacket and today there have been over fifty Lebowski Fests in over thirty cities.

**JH:** *Can you describe your first experience with* The Big Lebowski *for the readers? How did it affect you?*

**WR:** I was almost indifferent to it the first time I saw it. After the third time, I fell in love. I was completely smitten with it and found myself obsessively quoting dialogue and giggling every time. The movie gets better every time I watch it and I have seen it over a hundred times and it still makes me laugh out loud, which I don't know how to explain.

**JH:** *Who is your favourite* Lebowski *character? Why?*

**WR:** Walter is my favourite. He is the most ridiculous and has the best lines.

**JH:** *What sets* Lebowski *fans apart from other followers of cult films and series?*

**WR:** *Lebowski* fans, also known as 'Achievers', are great people. They are smart. A little nerdy but still like to party. It's a bit nerdy like a *Star Trek* convention but with more drinking and bowling. The Coen brothers are not for dummies. Yes, the Achievers, and proud we are of all of them.

**JH:** *Would you consider yourselves as devoted as some of the Achievers in Eddie Chung's film? The Walrus?*

**WR:** Absolutely. I still adore this movie with all my heart and find it to be a pleasure and an honour to travel the country celebrating with fellow fans.

**JH:** *What are your feelings about the movie? Do you think it will weather the test of time?*

**WR:** No doubt about it, it will be recognized as one of the greatest movies of all time. It gets better and better with each viewing and new fans are born every day.

**JH:** *Do you see Lebowski Fest continuing to grow?*

**WR:** Lebowski Fest seems to have no end in sight. We see lots of regulars but we also see lots of new fans. Everyone is very friendly and welcoming. It's a great feeling to attend a Lebowski Fest and people will always want to have a blast with good people. Lebowski Fest is a fan-driven event unlike traditional concerts where thousands of people are watching a few people onstage. At Lebowski Fest, the Achievers are the stars of the show and everyone wants to take pictures together and quote lines.

**JH:** *How would you describe* Lebowski*'s influence on pop culture/television?*

**WR:** It shows up everywhere in lines of dialogue in sitcoms, cartoons, art, etc. It is an integral part of American pop culture.

**JH:** *How would you describe international fans versus American fans? Which country appears to achieve the most in terms of fandom?*

**WR:** The UK Fest certainly had a more rowdy bunch. The Europeans are not as restrained as the American fans which would put them high in the running for most unrestrained worldwide.

**JH:** *Have the Coen brothers ever attended a Lebowski Fest? If not, do you* *think they will?*

**WR:** They have not, yet. They did let us borrow the marmot prop one year and I ran into Joel Coen and his wife Frances McDormand in Louisville recently while they were on a road trip. Frances said if we made it to 25 years they might come, so there's that. They seemed genuinely relieved that I wasn't an absolute lunatic.

**JH:** *Are you a Dudeist? If so, can you explain the philosophy to the readers briefly?*

**WR:** I'm a nihilist but I dig Dudeism.

**JH:** *Eddie Chung's film,* The Achievers *(2009), had a kind of somber tone regarding the fans; is that a reflection of the Achievers themselves or a signal of the deterioration of the founding members of Lebowski Fest?*

**WR:** I was disappointed by the tone of that film as Lebowski Fest is such a fun and joyous experience. I really think that that film missed the most important point of Lebowski Fest and the fans of the film as these gatherings are like family reunions where fans meet and form lifelong connections. I am sad that some of the original Achievers aren't into the event anymore as they helped build it and it is largely unchanged. I'm holding out hope that they will one day return.

**JH:** *Do you think there should be a sequel [to* The Big Lebowski*]? Why, or why not?*

**WR:** Absolutely not. That is not the Coens' style and they have even said as much. *The Big Lebowski* is sacred script and fans resent even the smallest detail being changed. It is pure gold and can never be improved or added to. If some studio tried to circumvent the Coens on this it would be a fucking travesty.

**JH:** *Does Lebowski Fest generate enough revenue to keep the fires burning?*

**WR:** Our goal is to bring in enough to cover the cost of the event and keep it going to the next. We created this event as fans with fans in mind and are always asking 'Is this something I like?' and 'Does this seem fair?' I manage a retail store, WHY Louisville, as my day job.

**JH:** *Have you ever bowled a perfect game?*

**WR:** Ha! Not even close. I'm lucky to make it halfway to 300. I think my best game is 186. The Achievers are better drinkers than they are bowlers.

**JH:** *What is your favourite scene of the film? Why?*

**WR:** This is an impossible thing to answer as I truly adore every frame and favourite lines/scenes change all the time. If forced to choose, I would have to go with the Jesus's first time on-screen where he licks the ball, does the dance and the Gypsy Kings's 'Hotel California' (1988) kicks in. I think that is possibly the best 30 seconds in cinematic history and every time we screen the film at Lebowski Fest, the crowd erupts during that scene as if it was a band playing their hit song.

'NIHILISTS! FUCK ME.
I MEAN, SAY WHAT
YOU WANT
ABOUT THE TENETS
OF NATIONAL
SOCIALISM, DUDE,
AT LEAST IT'S AN
ETHOS.'

**WALTER SOBCHEK**

Chapter
3

# 'If You Will It, It Is No Dream': Lebowski Fest and Cult Fandom

Jeremy Hehl

→ **Great achievements in human history are generally recognized as acts of magnanimous contrivance - bold feats with strokes of triumph and victory. *The Big Lebowski* was a triumph; the film tripled its budget in the box office, generated a cultural following, a loyal and admiring viewership, and even an incredibly slow-growing religion.**

*Fig. 1: The Dude, awestruck at the condition his film is in after fifteen years*

For Lebowski there was no explosion of fandom immediately after the release of the film - sure it generated a tremendous amount of buzz for the Coen brothers, who were still reaping the accolades from their Academy Award-winning film ***Fargo*** (1996).
The audience is often a harsh mistress, and expectations being as fleeting and unpredictable as they are, *The Big Lebowski* found itself in a pool full of comparative contrasts with *Fargo*. Today the films are mutually distinct, and in the end the Dude achieved the nominal recognition of the movie-going public. Sobchakian aphorisms very quickly began to permeate verbal popular culture, nihilists everywhere rejoiced momentarily and then gave up, and a new film fandom was born, a type of fandom which celebrates people as they are. It remains politically neutral, goes bowling and bangs back Caucasians - a cultural group referring to itself abidingly as 'Achievers'.

Upon setting out in search of clarification of the preferred nomenclature for Lebowski fans I was eagerly met with all types of fansites, fanart and merchandise on the Internet. People everywhere seem to love the movie. The fanfare during the film's initial release in 1998 felt lacklustre when compared to the current and ever-growing number of people who have embraced the Dude. The diehard may claim they see deeper meaning in the film's subtexts, when in reality most are probably just as confused as the

**'If You Will It, It Is No Dream': Lebowski Fest and Cult Fandom**
Jeremy Hehl

Fig. 2: Julianne Moore and Jeff Bridges

Dude was when he was getting his head dunked in the toilet. The meaning of the film is delightfully relativistic. Interpretation is the film's best friend; it's easy for a viewer to identify with at least one of the characters in the cast. The Dude is a man of absolute contentment - a man who embraces the lifestyle most of us want, but seldom allow ourselves to 'achieve'.

In 1970 radical anti-Vietnam protests led by Michael Lerner kicked off at the University of Washington - the movement dubbed itself the Seattle Liberation Front. The 'Seattle Seven' as they came to be known earned their titles by being charged with inciting a riot at a Seattle courthouse. Of these seven people, one in particular became of primary interest to the research conducted herein: Jeff Dowd. A quick search on Wikipedia reveals a briskly jotted article on his sanctimonious crowning as the real-life inspiration for the Dude's character in *The Big Lebowski*. But could it really be that simple? A political activist from Seattle inspired one of the greatest cult icons of the twentieth and twenty-first centuries?

It has to be deeper than that, and in order to achieve an understanding of the people driving the fandom of the movie (in small but serious ways) I conducted a series of interviews with one of the founders of Lebowski Fest, first held 12 October 2002. I was lucky enough to get in contact with Founding Dude Will Russell, who closed his responses to me with 'Abidingly, Will'. With the assistance of fellow Founding Dude Scott Shuffitt, the inaugural event was held in a Baptist-run bowling alley which did not allow cussing or drinking, but 150 people showed up and 'had a blast'. The numbers of attendees would swell at future events, and the Lebowski Fest now takes place five to six times a

*Fig. 3: All the Dudes congregate at Lebowski Fest*

year, usually drawing around a thousand people with the flagship Fest in Louisville drawing close to two thousand Achievers. I asked Russell what he thought was most important to Lebowski fans – was it the expansion of the viewership of the film? Or was it something deeper, like messages or mythos? But his responses in regard to Lebowski fandom were more along the lines of 'having a blast, White Russians, costumes, bowling and "shomer-fucking-Shabbos"'. Indeed the plot of the film is ultimately unimportant, and taking what Will means in his context is quite simple – the celebration is in the characters, the music, the dialogue and the masterful visual styling of the Coen brothers. When I asked Russell a blunt question (pun intended) regarding marijuana advocacy and the inclination of some to pin that currently contentious social issue on the Dude, he tersely noted that the festival doesn't 'endorse or oppose anything in particular, other than *The Big Lebowski*'. Maybe that question was unfair, but it begs consideration when a multitude of those achieving true Dudeism seek to emulate the existence of Jeff Lebowski. Am I the only one who gives a shit about the rules? Ultimately, Lebowski Fest is really a social gathering where people of 'like-minded disposition' get together and celebrate the film and its beautiful complexities and simple subtleties.

I have yet to attend a Lebowski Fest, but I will. Not for the spectacle, I've had that, but for the communal experience. There is something really genuine about these fans, the Achievers. Some are likely progressively-minded Dude-types, while others are conservative, gun-toting Walters, but all are fans of *The Big Lebowski*. Alas, there is something still quite sad about being an Achiever – it's like the permanent social niche that *The Rocky Horror Picture Show* (Jim Sharman, 1975) carved out for its adherents. People get together, recreate the scenarios in the film and imagine they are part of the filmic universe. 'Normal' society tells us to pity these people – to mock their fandom in a consternating manner – to demand that they snap back into reality and function normally. But, where's the fun in that?

American counter-culture will rapidly consume and promote anything that represents fringe society. Often, as Russell was quick to point out, a film has to first be rejected by the mainstream in order to develop a cult following, as evident in the aftermarket successes of *Brazil* (Terry Gilliam, 1985), *The Princess Bride* (Rob Reiner, 1987), *The Shawshank Redemption* (Frank Darabont, 1994) and even *Donnie Darko* (Richard Kelly, 2001). All of these films generated uninspired box office totals but accumulated

**'If You Will It, It Is No Dream': Lebowski Fest and Cult Fandom**
Jeremy Hehl

*Fig. 4: Jeff Dowd offers a toast with Scott Shuffitt in the background*

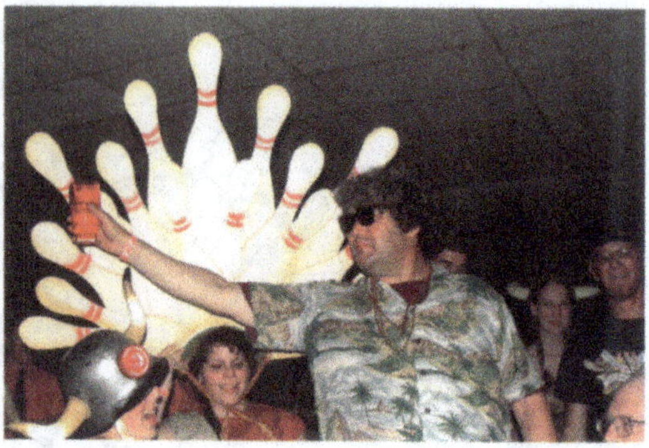

massive cult followings during the aftermarket phase of their release.

Yet, isn't there something kind of morose about cult film fandom? Don't cult films have to be repetitiously replayed in order to garner the support they require to remain 'cult' in identity? There is no mistaking that *The Big Lebowski* has achieved international recognition due to its persistent 'replay culture', and the film has been shown to audiences nationwide in repertory screenings enabling it to garner the recognition it deserves. The film strangely appeals to people from all stripes: druggies, non-druggies, students and academics, rock band musicians, sports figures, journalists, corporate achievers, Vietnam veterans and the ex-hippies of the world.

The crowd at these events is surprisingly raucous, and probably unimaginably stoned. The several clips I perused on YouTube suggest that the crowd gets as personally invested in characterization as they do with the spectacle. They often shout back at the screen, chanting dialogue together. They openly abide drinking and marijuana use, and view the mood-altering as a rite associated with a true engagement of the film. Lebowski Fest, which has its roots in the midnight movie craze of the 1970s, is arguably akin to the popularity of cosplay at midnight debuts for sci-fi and superhero films today. The *Lebowski* cultus exists because the festival provides the comfort of acceptable social paradigms in order to justify its existence; it has been institutionalized and propped up against legitimate academic research, and now cultural groups and gatherings.

It is the aftermarket which pointedly determines the legacy of films like *The Big Lebowski*. The 'cult boom' is likely linked to the variety of portals through which people are today consuming media, and many new fans have become aware of the film through academic settings. Since the Internet boom of the mid-1990s, our experiences in media consumption have started to bridge across several platforms. Because of this modal form of viewership, the cult of the Achiever, like many film cults before it, is able to grow efficiently without the need for cinematic re-release. When consumption of the film becomes available in several distinct flavours, it becomes possible for the fan base to grow in dynamic ways. Dudeism is spreading like a religion, and it is taking on developmental and socially impactful issues like 'achieving something during your life'. Social ethos draws its strengths from cultural mythos – after watching *The Big Lebowski*, who doesn't want to access their inner Dude?

The Dude, in a contemporary culture rooted in memes, represents the perfect hero. He takes all things with a grain of salt, living through detachment as would the Buddha or others of his ilk. The neo-noir style in which the Coen brothers revel in here unleashes a bevy of elements that empowers a film rooted in stoner culture. A marmot in a bathtub, references to acid flashbacks and casual pot-use all make the film completely accessible for those who support mind-altering substances. Counter-cultural associations with drug use (alcohol included) are especially popular in university settings. The

*Fig. 5: 10th Annual Lebowski Fest poster*

'Lebowski Challenge' involves matching the Dude Caucasian for Caucasian throughout the film – it's a harrowing gauntlet, but I was able to do it … for research.

Surrealism (as it goes), especially when honed into a sharp edge, offers the possibility of varying types of interpretation. Our tastes as digital consumers have changed in an era in which *everything* is available somewhere on the Internet. The public is comfortable with the benign fringes of society, and it remains easier than ever to explore oddities in our media-saturated world. Mastery of dialogue, nihilists, smoking pot in forbidden places, the feminist avant-garde, iron lungs and edited-for-television lines ('See what happens when you find a stranger in the Alps?') all make for a meme-ready film aimed almost perfectly at the modern (r)evolution. It might be prudent to wager and say that *The Big Lebowski* has created its own distinct counter-culture, steeped in eastern philosophical detachment, marijuana advocacy and celebration of mediocrity.

Dudeism celebrates apathetic solidarity, and that's not necessarily a bad thing. As Jeff Bridges said at the Lebowski Fest in New York in 2009, 'That's just, like, your opinion, man.' He was quoting one his favourite lines in the film, but the line he chose perfectly encapsulates the pervasive mentality and stigma surrounding the film, especially when Achievers are sitting in the balcony lighting up joints during a cast and crew press conference. The Coen brothers are masters of idiosyncratic films bolstered by appealing and genuine oddball characters. Much to their credit they have cultivated a roster of hyper-genuine characters played by stars: H. I. McDunnough (Nicolas Cage) in *Raising Arizona* (1987), Marge Gunderson (Frances McDormand) in *Fargo*, the indomitable Everett McGill (George Clooney) in *O Brother Where Art Thou* (2000), in addition to Bridges's Dude. The Dude and Jeff Bridges at this point are almost indistinguishable – my sister now refers to the actor as Jeffrey Lebowski. If nothing else, the trademark jelly sandals Jeff wears in real life are a confirmation of his own 'Dude-ness'.

The most dominant aspect for the Achiever collective remains the replay value of the film, the recycled and often repurposed transitional dialogue which offers new tidbits with each viewing, the new criterion by which all neo-noir farcical comedies must be judged … or at least those which also involve a lot of bowling. It is replay culture that continues to offer shelter to the fledgling Lebowski fan base. In a way, the Dude is always there for the viewer, never intrusive, always going with the flow. Sure he has his share of bad days, but in the end he finds a solution to his ever-cascading series of problems – all the while wanting nothing to do with any of it. It is that nonchalant, detached attitude which resonates a nearly Buddhist sense of calm and reflects back upon the primarily white male fan-base in a calming, reassuring effort to assuage feelings of negative self-worth and self-loathing. In other words: the Dude abides, so why shouldn't I?

I have never heard a word of disdain about the film beyond some people (you know the type) who 'just don't get it'. I, for one, think the world needs more Dudes. I think the greatest tragedy in pushing the fandom of a film or series too far in terms of cult mentality is when it begins to damage the fabric of understanding for the casual audience. The art of a film, especially a sleeper masterpiece like *The Big Lebowski*, gets lost in the hustle and bustle of the fandom machine – people have a tendency to over-consume whatever mythos they buy into. Over-emulation and over-personification 'achieve' nothing.

Still there remains something intrinsically beautiful about the film and its ability to maintain an audience. The Achievers don't watch the film in order to recreate and participate in the universe – they *are* the universe. The multifaceted world of replay culture continues to diversify. Repeated viewing of the film creates aesthetic changes and offer Achievers a compelling source of pleasure; repetition calls attention to previously unnoticed elements of the film and creates a continuity and admeasurement seldom found in the initial viewing, as both the familiar and the novel bring added pleasure.

That is not to say that there isn't sometimes a darker side to *Lebowski* fandom, sometimes 'darker'n a black steer's tookus on a moonless prairie night', as evident in Eddie Chung's documentary *The Achievers: The Story of the Lebowski Fans* (2009). While it solidifies the cultural stock of the fan base and further promotes the film through social contexts, it reveals how some of the people who call themselves 'Achievers' are just the opposite. We are welcomed into Stormy's personal life as she describes her online business of creating *Time* 'Person of the Year' mirrors and selling them on the Internet. Obsessed with winning a first-place trophy at one of the permanent fixtures of Lebowski Fest(s), the trivia contest, the documentary opens with her crushing reaction to a second place finish, all the while dressed in a walrus costume (from Donny's 'I am the walrus' confusion). We become astutely aware of the meaning the film and her participation in this fan-driven cultural group has taken in her life. Chung ably highlights the idolatry surrounding even characters of the films with no lines. Fans clamour for autographs and pictures, swoon at the appearances of minor characters in the film and are enraptured at the sight of Bridges (with his band) at the 2005 Lebowski Fest in Los Angeles.

Indeed, there are several scenes of Lebowski Fests over the years (some are the more creative costumes include the 'camel-fuckers' and the 'jerkoff manual'), but numerous individuals are interviewed in the 70-minute documentary, including original forum members, the Founding Dudes, as well as Bridges and actors who are onscreen but have no lines. The film covers the full range of Lebowski fans – from the casual participant to the uber-obsessed fan. But Chung often returns to Stormy – she is the heart of the film. When we see her trivia triumph at the following year's Lebowski Fest, we are happy for her, but the director's presentation of her elation markedly draws attention to how sad the event is. She trembles as she holds the trophy, looks as if she is about to cry, and a slow fade to black signals the lasting impression I believe Chung is hoping to impart. All that is good fades to black. Nothing about *The Achievers* is overtly negative, and the overarching feeling of the film is one of celebration, but Stormy's obsession with-achieving the title of trivia champion becomes a sad display of compulsive infatuation. Chung is clearly an Achiever himself and his goal does not appear to be the ridicule of the Lebowski fan base, rather, the purpose of the film is one of exploration and curiosity. But for the casual viewer, the idiosyncrasies of some of the diehard fans force the viewer into a position of judgment regardless of our personal level of fandom or Dudeness.

In what appears to be a coup directed at the standardized Hollywood distribution model, *The Big Lebowski* has become one of those aftermarket distribution phenomena - *Office Space* (Mike Judge, 1999) and *Half Baked* (Tamra Davis, 1998) also merit attention - that creates its loyal following through public and private replay. It gains cult traction through a collective sense of taking it easy. The film beautifies the toil of life - even the Stranger tells us that everything works out for the Dude. Founding Dudes Will Russell and Scott Shuffitt must be aware of the film's international fandom and thus considering holding Fests outside of the Anglo-American world. Now over 15 years old, *The Big Lebowski* seems to lose no steam, continuing to find purchase in the hearts of Dudeist converts, and making an Achiever out of all of us ... aw look at me, I'm ramblin' again. It may be just like, *my* opinion, man, but I like to think there's a little Lebowski inside each and every one of us. ●

**GO FURTHER**

**Extracts/Essays/Articles**

'Becoming Cult: *The Big Lebowski*, Replay Culture and Male Fans'
Barbara Klinger
In *Screen*. 51: 1 (2010), pp. 1–20.

**Film/Television**

*The Achievers: The Story of the Lebowski Fans*, Eddie Chung, dir. (USA: K-Man Productions, 2009)

**Online**

*Lebowski Fest*, www.lebowskifest.com

Chapter
4

# That Shirt Really Ties the Room Together: The Lebowski Legacy of Cultural Artefacts

Andrew Howe

→ **Following its 1998 release, a loyal fan base quickly grew up around *The Big Lebowski*, celebrating its quirky characters and plot developments. The film managed to capture the zeitgeist of the moment, linking the 1960s through the post-hippie character of the Dude to the late 1990s with its celebration of slacker culture and grunge rock. More surprising, however, was the staying power of this fan base, as the film quickly acquired cult status. It joined a very short list of cinematic and television works whose fame and popularity only seemed to grow more pronounced over time.**

Films such as *Night of the Living Dead* (George A. Romero, 1968) and *The Rocky Horror Picture Show* (Jim Sharman, 1975), and television shows including *Star Trek* (Gene Rodenberry, NBC, 1966–69) and *Twin Peaks* (David Lynch and Mark Frost, ABC, 1990–91), enjoyed life long after their runs had ended, kept culturally current by large numbers of dedicated fans who would not let the characters and plotlines and quotations fade into obscurity. There are several reasons as to why *The Big Lebowski* secured such a loyal and diverse fan base. That the film was charmingly idiosyncratic could not be denied, and it was released during a period when the Coen brothers were at the height of their creative powers. *Lebowski* was sandwiched in between the critically acclaimed *Fargo* (1996), the film that established the brothers as more than artsy genre film-makers, and *O Brother, Where Art Thou?* (2000), an ambitious retelling of *The Odyssey* critically acclaimed not only for its film-making, but also its use of music. The Coen brothers had already become known for their ability to transform genres in interesting and quirky ways, but in their decision to introduce a modern counter-culture hero to the tried-and-true formula of Raymond Chandler's acerbically witty detective Philip Marlowe, they had found a rare combination. For these reasons and others, *The Big Lebowski* continues to enjoy a high level of cultural resonance to this day. The film's continued status as iconic cult cinema is evident in the cultural objects caught up in its orbit, in the subsequent ephemera that have, in many ways, grown beyond their initial design to take on lives of their own. These artefacts exist at a complex nexus of fan culture, fashion and economics, establishing a legacy of cultural relevance that continues to impact popular media.

The dedicated group of fans venerating this cult film has helped keep it alive, in part, by creating and driving an online market of cultural artefacts associated with the more popular elements of the film. T-shirts, bumper stickers, mugs, action figures, and other objects continue to mediate cultural consciousness, impacting even those who have never seen the film. Indeed, in my 'Hollywood and American History' course, I recently put up a picture of the Dude and asked the students about his identity. Although the film was released when most of these students were 5 to 6 years old, and only two students acknowledged having seen the film, the majority recognized the image and about half correctly identified the character as having 'something to do with a dude'. Anecdotes aside, the vast number of Lebowski-themed items for sale on the second-hand website eBay – with the number ranging between 3,000 and 5,000, more than half of these within the clothing section – illustrates the manner in which such items continue to be bought and sold in large quantities. Some of these collectibles were officially sanctioned objects generated during the lead-up to and immediately following the film's 1998 release, while others have been subsequently created for anniversaries or fan conventions. Although the Internet was in existence prior to 1998, it was during the late 1990s that this innovation really took off as a cultural force. It is probably no coincidence that a technology that was quickly embraced by the coveted 18–35-year-old demographic was employed to build interest in the film and later serve as a market-

## That Shirt Really Ties the Room Together: The Lebowski Legacy of Cultural Artefacts

Andrew Howe

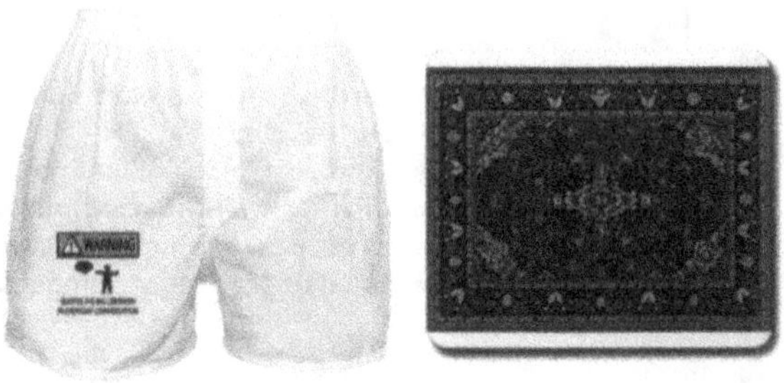

*Fig. 1-2: Lebowski boxers; the rug mousepad, for Achievers who really want to tie their workspace together*

place for those seeking to demonstrate fan loyalty by purchasing and displaying items linked to the film. In the years following the 1998 release, other artefacts were subsequently created by graphic designers seeking to cash in upon the film's continuing popularity, with fans eager to buy the latest Lebowski-inspired T-shirt, exhibiting their continued loyalty through their sartorial choices. The marriage between fan demand and the technological immediacy of the Internet has born a market-driven proliferation of artefacts that has served to advance *Lebowski* iconography. An interesting, but perhaps not too surprising, dimension of this phenomenon has been that fan selection, both in the design and consumption of such memorabilia, has served to mediate which characters, quotes, and other aspects of the film have maintained, or even grown in, their cultural currency.

For analysis, such artefacts can be divided into object type. Articles of clothing, such as T-shirts and sweatshirts, predominate upon such online stores and second-hand sites. CafePress even has nine different Lebowski-inspired pairs of underwear for sale, one of which proclaims 'Warning! Quotes the Big Lebowski in everyday conversation'. However, one can also find fashion accessories such as necklaces or other pieces of jewellery as well as utilitarian objects such as coffee mugs, bowling-ball bags, or even mousepads featuring film-related things such as the Dude's rug. Instead of employing these divisions for analysis, this chapter will instead focus upon artefact content, including such categories as characters, quotations and themes. It is no surprise that Jeffrey Lebowski (Jeff Bridges), most often known as the Dude, predominates when it comes to characters that adorn such artefacts. Surprising, however, is the prevalence of Walter Sobchak (John Goodman), who runs a very close second when it comes to popularity, at least as determined by the vast number of T-shirts, mugs, and other objects upon which his visage and/or quotations appear. Even though Walter is the Dude's close friend, the former exists in the narrative as a counterpoint to the title character. Walter is aggressive, bellicose and not hesitant to employ weaponry in order to get his way, all things that run counter to the Dude's philosophies. As an impulsive, violent and anti-PC character who is fashioned as one of the protagonists of the film (and, according to Ronald Bergan, based upon director/screenwriter John Milius), and in his quirky construction as a bowling-obsessed, Jewish convert, Vietnam vet, Walter was given a foundation by the Coen brothers to elevate him above the other quirky figures populating the film. However, it is the character's witty, and peculiar, lines of dialogue, delivered so well by Goodman, that transform Walter into the cult character of this cult film.

One T-shirt, which depicts Walter's face with the quote 'I don't roll on Shabbos', simultaneously brings together Walter's Jewish faith and interest in bowling, as well as the pastime of smoking marijuana. Another commonly seen T-shirt, which depicts Walter's head and shoulders and the phrase 'You are entering a world of pain', references the character's bellicose nature and over-the-top humour. If anything, the character of Walter Sobchak has become more popular in the fifteen years following the film's

*Fig. 3-5: Various T-shirts inspired by Walter*

release than he was at the time. His character has been incorporated into memes that gained cultural traction well after 1998, as is evidenced by a mashup of one of his more popular quotes, 'Calmer than you are', and the British wartime advice to 'Keep Calm and Carry On'. Although this phrase was employed on World War II propaganda posters, it experienced resurgence in popularity in the decade following the film's release, when a British bookstore found an old poster and began selling facsimiles. The irony here is that violent, impulsive Walter Sobchak is anything but the British picture of composure and detachment, and that shortly before uttering this phrase he brandishes a firearm!

Of course, the Dude is the character that appears upon the largest portion of the memorabilia associated with the film. He is everything that Walter is not, existing as a link to the domestic counter-culture of the 1960s rather than the violence and belligerence that was American foreign policy in Vietnam and other locations. The conservative policies of the Reagan administration resulted in a counter-culture that culminated with the advent of 'grunge rock' and that would be memorialized in 1991 with productions in three different mediums: Nirvana's song 'Smells Like Teen Spirit', Richard Linklater's film *Slackers*, and Douglas Coupland's book *Generation X: Tales for an Accelerated Culture*. The ensuing decade would be one of unprecedented wealth in American society, typified by startup Internet and tech companies and a bull financial market that would allow the United States to consistently play down the national debt. As is often the case during times of economic plenty, the counter-culture began to fade in both engagement and relevance. It was during the end of this period when *The Big Lebowski* was released, making it all the more impressive for its success. However, the film had several things going for it. In linking the open-minded rebelliousness of youth during the 1960s in the aging hippie the Dude to a new form of counter-culture so fresh in viewers' minds, the film was able to appeal to Baby Boomers and Gen Xers alike.

Furthermore, a film about an unassuming, non-judgmental character such as the Dude would have likely appealed to an audience weary of the highly inflammatory rhetoric and political division that accompanied President Bill Clinton's second term in office. Indeed, the Monica Lewinsky scandal broke about six weeks prior to the film's release, and by the end of the year the country had witnessed only the second presidential impeachment in its history. To Americans sick of politics and the divisiveness they saw around them, the Dude's studied lack of political involvement upon any level was quite attractive. Some artefacts, such as a T-shirt allusion to Shepard Fairey's famous Obama 'Hope' poster, reference this political angle. Although less than 10 years old, Fairey's poster has been used to advance a variety of politically-motivated memes, most recently a series of posters that reference the controversy surrounding the collection of private telephone and e-mail communication by the National Security Agency, with captions such as 'Yes We Scan ... Deal With It!' and 'Yes We Can ... Read Your Emails'. In the *Lebowski* version, the red-and-blue visage of the Dude is accompanied by the word 'Abide', referencing the resilience and dependability attributed to the character

*Fig. 6-8: Shephard Fairey-inspired 'Abide' T-shirt; Mug mashup with* Game of Thrones*; Donny action figure*

by the film's narrator. In another mashup, a mug depicting the Dude sitting upon the Iron Throne, an iconic symbol from the popular book (George R. R. Martin, 1996) and its television adaptation *Game of Thrones* (David Benioff and D. B. Weiss, HBO, 2011- ), is both illustrative and nonsensical, simultaneously establishing the continued cultural relevance of *The Big Lebowski* in linking it to a popular, and current, artistic project, while straining credulity and moving well beyond irony in the fact that the Dude, a pacifist who avoids conflict at all costs and who has no desire for power, should end up surviving George R. R. Martin's world of bloody, internecine warfare and political intrigue. Surprisingly, not too many other characters from the Lebowski universe are depicted upon the cultural artefacts associated with the film. Perhaps this is because the Dude and Walter exist on such opposite ends of the spectrum, and that such a quirky film elicits extreme depictions. Or, perhaps it is due to the fact that these two characters are given the funniest and most memorable lines of dialogue. Whatever the reason, potential buyers have to run searches for specific characters or else sift through pages of online memorabilia. There are, however, a few secondary characters that are more prevalent than others. T-shirts or other objects featuring Jesus Quintana (John Turturro) are not uncommon, despite the fact that this character is fairly minor to the inner workings of the film's plot. Perhaps this popularity is due to Turturro's excellence in filling, even dominating, each scene in which he appears, mostly through his memorable physicality. From licking or shining his bowling ball to performing a celebratory dance following a strike to his habit of referring to himself in the third person as 'the Jesus', replete with a hard 'J' Anglo pronunciation, Turturro's Quintana is simply unforgettable.

It is also possible to find objects associated with the naive and easy going Theodore (Donny) Kerabatsos (Steve Buscemi), who much like Jesus enters the film upon the level of comic relief, albeit in a much different fashion. Even though they are friends, Donny often serves as whipping boy to Walter's belligerence. Much of the time Donny appears stoned and out of it, and the fast-paced world in which the Dude, and by extension his friends, is forced to inhabit, seems to be too much for this character. Even though merchandise featuring him is not too common, Donny, as well as some of his notable quotations, appears upon T-shirts and mugs, and he even has his own bobble head and action figure. Accessorized with a beer bottle and hamburger, the action figure contains a button that if pushed will randomly select one of five notable quotes by this character, including 'Man, I'm throwing rocks tonight!' and 'He peed on The Dude's rug'. It is interesting to note that Jesus and Donny appear upon such objects with more frequency than those who are more central to the overall plot, including figures such as Maude Lebowski (Julianne Moore), Bunny Lebowski (Tara Reid) and the other Jeffrey Lebowski (David Huddleston). Whereas these characters are more important to the machinations of the film's narrative, they lack the visceral humour that perhaps dictates which of the characters beyond the Dude and Walter are more popular with collecting audiences (Maude is portrayed in a fairly humorous light, but the comedy here is more

Fig. 9: Jesus costume with bowling bag

intellectual in nature, and therefore elitist). Supporting this hypothesis is that the German Nihilists (Flea, Peter Stormare and Torsten Voges), who enjoy precious little but utterly hilarious screen time, enjoy several T-shirts and other objects that feature them.

Although the vast majority of fan-based *Lebowski* accessorizing is distinctly character-driven, there are references to group identifications. Pins, badges, bumper stickers, and even articles of clothing when displayed proclaim allegiance to certain groups that exist within the film's narrative. For instance one can wear a shirt identifying themselves as a 'Little Lebowski Urban Achiever', part of the film's backstory establishing the Big Lebowski, despite his relative disengagement from society, as philanthropic, evidenced by the trophies he won by working with disadvantaged youth. Likewise, in the online store Fantasy Toyland, one can identify as a member of Jesus Quintana's bowling team by purchasing a purple 'Big Lebowski Jesus Bowling Costume', which runs $74.95 for shirt and slacks, and with an optional add-on of a purple 'Jesus Bowling Bag' for $21.95. A final marker of belonging involves objects that affiliate the bearer with Dudeism, 'the slowest-growing religion in the world'. Sporting a purple and white ying-yang logo that references a bowling ball in that three holes appear upon each of the heads, and with wisdom and advice collected within an official *Abide Guide*, Dudeism is associated with numerous artefacts from which its proponents can select by going to the website's online store. Particular markers of belonging to this religion can be proudly displayed, such as the certificate of ordination for the official church associated with Dudeism, the Church of the Latter-Day Dude. Over 150,000 people worldwide have been ordained by this church, and Dudeist Priests are eligible to perform wedding ceremonies in most state and county jurisdictions across the United States. Like most online ordination sites, this one has a vow: 'I vow to uphold the principles of Dudeism: To just take it easy, to be *dude* (easygoing) to everyone I meet, and to keep my mind limber.' Those who complete the online form are sent laminated certificates that can be framed and hung upon the wall like a diploma. Unlike T-shirts that display the visage of a single character, such artefacts are less about celebrating singular identifications and more about group identity. Accompanying the rise of the Internet was the rise in popularity of fanfiction, a phenomenon whereby writers or artists injected their own plotlines or characters into the fictional worlds they had grown to love, sharing these stories with like-minded others. Bumper stickers and T-shirts, many of which were designed by fans, serve to highlight the politics of belonging by forming attachments upon a group register, where fans are able to feel a part of something larger than if they had simply worn a shirt displaying their favourite character. Fan culture, consumption and fashion are thus combined with group identity, introducing exclusivity into the equation.

Many of the items referenced earlier in this chapter under character and group iden-

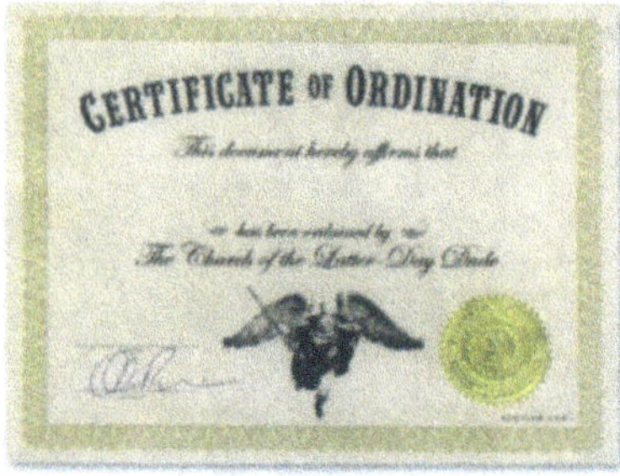


*Fig. 10: Dudeism ordination certificate*

tifications have involved witty or quirky quotations culled from the film. It is not uncommon, however, to see such quotes devoid of any context as to who spoke the line. Although the term 'dude' extends back in common usage to the late nineteenth century, and the term was common during the late 1980s with the emergence of a slacker counter-culture, many of the occurrences in today's society refer to *The Big Lebowski*. Invariably, mugs or T-shirts that feature this word are indeed referencing this film. Some of these, such as the bumper stickers that read 'The Dude Abides', link themselves inexorably to the film, even for those who may not have ever seen it. Some of the quotes leave no doubt as to the origin of the phrase, even if the casual fan has forgotten the context surrounding the quote. Others, such as the bumper sticker that reads: 'Well, that's just, like, your opinion, man ...' may not be attributable to the film by the casual fan. However, the laid-back, hippie/slacker diction and verbiage (full of pauses, the temporizing use of 'like', and ending the thought with 'man') would indicate the open-minded and extremely laid back nature of the Dude. Quintessentially, there is a T-shirt for sale on numerous sites dedicated solely to the film's most famous quotes. Dubbed the 'Quote T-Shirt', fans can purchase one shirt with twenty of the film's most memorable lines instead of twenty different shirts.

Internet stores such as CafePress sell new items, many of them recently designed, and second-hand sites such as eBay resell such items. There is a third group of artefacts, however, that can be found in second-hand markets, both in forums such as eBay but also on more exclusive sites: signed memorabilia. The intensely loyal fan base and cult interest in the film has resulted in festivals and conventions where fans are given the chance to interact, even if only briefly, with the actors. Many fans keep the item for which they stood in line to have signed, although some part with it due to financial hardship. Many of these are publicity photographs, either stills from the film itself or actor publicity shots put out by the studios. Others, however, are from photographs taken behind the scenes. Most such artefacts are signed solely by the actor depicted, but on occasion multiple individuals from the cast will sign an object, often at a convention. For instance, at the time of this writing a poster depicting part of the dream sequence where the Dude teaches Maude to bowl was being sold on eBay. Normally, such a poster would have gone for $10, but this one was signed by Jeff Bridges and other cast members, and was listed with a price of $700. Such signed items are different from the types of artefacts examined earlier in this chapter in that they are not meant to be worn or otherwise showcased in public, often because the affixing of a signature lends increased significance to the item, either in its estimated financial worth or sentimental value.

The items discussed in this chapter, and the characters, quotations and issues they depict, are naturally only the tip of the iceberg when it comes to the universe of Lebowski memorabilia. Although the Dude and Walter certainly predominate, and T-shirts are responsible for more than half of the artefacts found online for sale, other characters are depicted and there is a whole list of different items upon which they appear. Although thematically this chapter has largely focused upon the elements of the counter-culture, there are numerous other elements represented in this memorabilia, from minor references to full blown mashups involving Michael Jordan, marijuana, Jesus Christ, Leonardo da Vinci, *South Park*, The Beatles and *Night of the Living Dead*, among others. Fifteen years after its release, *The Big Lebowski* still enjoys a level of cultural currency shared by few other films from the same time period. 'The Dude Abides' is a phrase seen and heard commonly in popular culture, and the concept of the Dude continues to be used as fodder for the Internet-driven world of memes. Festivals are held annually in Louisville, Kentucky and London, England, and other cities have had special conventions and midnight showings celebrating the film. Television shows such as the short-lived *Veronica Mars* (Rob Thomas, UPN, 2004-2007), itself a cult favourite, contain references to the film. The most notable example of the film's continued popularity, however, lies in the thousands of items perpetually for sale on the Internet, many of them second-hand in nature but with a continual stream of newly designed artefacts to add to the number and diversity of items celebrating *The Big Lebowski*. Whether it be through design or consumption, fans can celebrate the film and indicate their likes and affiliations through their sartorial choices. Such artefacts not only link *Lebowski* fans to the past, reminding them of the first time they saw the film, but also establish in the present a like-minded group, where a passer-by on the street might nod and smile upon seeing another's T shirt, in so doing forging a community that shares similar political and aesthetic sensibilities. ●

## GO FURTHER

### Books

*The Coen Brothers*
Ronald Bergan
(New York: Thunder's Mouth Press, 2000)

### Websites

CafePress, http://www.cafepress.com

Chapter
5

# Nihilistic Dudes: The Masculine Cult Figure in Fin de Siècle American Cinema

Keith Clavin

**→ When recalling the films that closed the twentieth century in American cinema, we (the editorial 'we') might immediately consider *Titanic* (James Cameron, 1997), *Saving Private Ryan* (Steven Spielberg, 1998), *The Matrix* (Andy and Larry Wachowski, 1999), *The Sixth Sense* (M. Night Shyamalan, 1999), or a host of other well-known productions.**

*Fig. 1: the Dude in TIME: The Dude's bewildered glare into a mirror of TIME magazine touches several thematic cornerstones. At once an 'everyman' and 90's slacker, The Dude keeps a foot in each territory*

However, an alternative set of movies can be remembered from that period as well, a subset of pieces that arrived in theatres around the same time and, although not always resultant in large box offices, have come to define a moment in aesthetic and cultural history for Americans.

*Fear and Loathing in Las Vegas* (Terry Gilliam, 1998), *Rushmore* (Wes Anderson, 1998), *The Big Lebowski* (1998), *Fight Club* (David Fincher, 1999) and *Donnie Darko* (Richard Kelly, 2001) helped to usher in the twenty-first-century films that prove difficult to classify in respect to their more renowned counterparts. These films walked an aesthetic line between large studio projects and independent, transgressive presentations. While all of them received wide release, the commercial performance of each would be called mixed at best. However, part of what makes these films notable is that the minimal fanfare surrounding their original appearances has given way to rather enthusiastic (and lasting) appreciation from the movie-going public. They have attained what is often referred to as 'cult' status and could be classified into the subgenres of late 'Gen-X', 'slacker' or even 'stoner' films, even if none of these labels do justice to the originality and subtle distinctions of these movies. They share thematic and formal traits that join them as a type in American popular cultural history by building upon the contradictions of the world from which they were born. At once sophisticated yet linear, alarming yet soothing and dramatic yet funny, they form a narrative of enchantment through the grotesque and irrational.

In the following pages I would like to examine *The Big Lebowski* as a type of case study within the tradition of marginalized, cult films I have just described. In addition to some of the basic similarities outlined above, at the centre of each movie is a male lead, whose performance carries the story and whose characterization espouses a counter-cultural masculinity. I believe their approaches to society and life are timely ones and have helped to define a generation's perspective on American masculinity. When Walter, in *Lebowski*, asks the Nihilists, 'Who's the fucking nihilist here?' the audience is left to assume that this is a rhetorical question with an obvious answer. However, when the comment is taken as part of an implicit philosophy within the film its meaning becomes much more difficult to unpack. While Walter and the Dude are eccentric and inimitable, they are also members of a particular group of characters whose representations tend to subvert mainstream moral values and display an indisposition towards traditional labour and production. Are they lazy slackers, existential nihilists or rebels within a corrupt system? Perhaps all of the above. In order to organize this somewhat spacious topic, I will split the discussion into two categories, which employ comedy and purposeful insubordination as a style of critique towards standard depictions of masculinity and reposition the slacker as a de facto cultural leader for the era. The first section will explain how the Dude keeps himself at an arm's length from mainstream society through a process of self-marginalization. The second section will engage what is at stake during this process in terms of an ethical critique of consumer and mainstream American values. Throughout, I will focus on *Lebowski* but draw parallels to other representations of alternative masculinity that appear within this particular subgenre from the late 1990s.

## 'Sometimes there's a man ...'

The Stranger (Sam Elliot) opens the film with an introduction of the Dude as a person 'in the running' for laziest in the world. While his description might be interpreted as less than complimentary, it ultimately reveals an admiration for someone who can live so fully as an outsider. This ability is what defines the masculine cult figure to a large extent and one that I would like to expand upon with the Dude and Max Fischer from Wes Anderson's *Rushmore*. Although from disparate demographic backgrounds, Max and the Dude share a number of traits that help to define them as paradigms for the masculine cult figure. In particular, their relationship to standard western institutions is strained in a manner that coincides with their styles of masculinity. The clash of responses to the question posed by Mr Lebowski ('the Big Lebowski'), 'What makes a man?' emphasizes the differences within each man's gender ideology. *Lebowski* is a highly masculine movie on all fronts, and the question of manhood and productivity weighs heavily on that theme.

Perhaps the most often quoted line from *Lebowski* involves the Dude explaining to the elder Lebowski that he does not consider himself 'Mr Lebowski'. 'You're Mr Lebowski. I'm the Dude. So that's what you call me. You know, that or, uh, His Dudeness, or uh, Duder, or El Duderino if you're not into the whole brevity thing'. Beyond the humour of the many nicknames, the exchange highlights an important distinction between official, formal language of business and productive society as spoken by Mr Lebowski and the Dude's marginalized, unofficial titles as dubbed not by society but by himself. The difference expounds upon a contradiction that the Dude's existence draws to the foreground. The audience is led to believe that Mr Lebowski is a self-made man, who has pulled himself up by his own bootstraps (despite not having the use of his legs), and constructed an empire of wealth and civic fame. As his wall of accomplishments proves, Mr Lebowski has been recognized for many accomplishments, not the least of which is meeting Nancy Reagan when she was 'First Lady of the nation'. Mr Lebowski embodies the traditional liberal spirit where value is gauged through employment, wealth and public acknowledgement. The Dude, however, intentionally avoids all such determinations. He claims to have gone to college, although he spent more time in 'administration buildings' than any place else. He simultaneously partakes in mainstream society (he pays his rent, calls the police when robbed, plays in bowling leagues) and self-marginalizes himself within those structures. What I mean by this is that he purposefully allows himself to be pressed towards the margins of power structures in order to avoid their oppressive forces and expose the shallowness of their constructions. For instance, when Mr Lebowski references the Dude's employment status (on several occasions) the

Fig. 2: Sadaam: In a manner befitting the film's tone, the great villain of the 1990s, Sadaam Hussein, appears in a cameo as handing out a pair of bowling shoes.

status (on several occasions) the responses he receives range from evasive to complete insensibility, 'What day is this?' The Dude's reactions to this subject matter display an innate disapproval of the 'manly man' approach that Mr Lebowski espouses.

In *Rushmore*, we find a similar ideological dynamic between Max and Herman Blume (Bill Murray), a millionaire business tycoon whose obnoxious twin sons attend Rushmore. While Blume proves to be a sympathetic character, his approach to success is to 'take dead aim at the rich kids'. But the real tension for Max derives from his relationship with Rushmore Academy, the school he has attended since first grade. He leads the French Club, edits the yearbook, captains the debate team, manages the lacrosse team, is a member of the Kung Fu Club, and participates in many other school associations. As he builds a portion of his resume through these activities he also fails out of the school due to a complete refusal to do actual schoolwork. On the one hand, he could be a model member of the Little Lebowski Urban Achievers. He is the son of an uneducated barber, very social and seemingly intelligent. However, he disdains the standard process of schooling, manipulating the bylaws of the school's regulations to avoid expulsion time after time. He shuns standard institutional learning and in the process creates his own, personal version of education. Self-learning through self-marginalization appears as a trend from the masculine cult figure. The method allows these cult characters to participate as non-participants, to be there without being an ingredient of the system of which they disapprove.

As the Stranger attempts to describe the Dude with the phrase 'sometimes there's a man ...' but trails off without finishing his thought, so does the masculine cult figure remain incomplete. The Dude himself demonstrates a similar lack of completion when, after he impregnates Maude and spits out his drink, declares, 'Let me explain something about the Dude ...' but never does. Max Fischer and the Dude offer performances of masculinity that are dependent upon defining themselves against a set of norms that remains in flux. He can never be fully formed other than being an 'other' to the productive, hard-working middle-class models of men and their behaviours; therefore the cult figure evolves and reappears from one generation to the next not unlike the traditional trickster figure. Often contradictory and difficult to understand, the seemingly irrational aspects of these characters are the very traits that make them important and unique.

**Nihilistic Dudes: The Masculine Cult Figure in Fin de Siècle American Cinema**
Keith Clavin

*Fig. 3: Walter and Smokey: Walter's pose, dress, and haircut clearly pay homage to Vietnam era snapshots and legends of GI cruelty.*

## 'The whole durn human comedy'

For a film that gives ample attention to nihilists and traces the comings and goings of an unemployed, socially detached protagonist, *Lebowski* peppers its dialogue with philosophical terms and ethical dilemmas. As Mr Lebowski serves as a foil to the Dude's unproductive nature, Walter serves as an ideological foil on many levels. His participation in the Vietnam conflict along with (an alleged) savvy approach to the kidnapping, and a tendency for loud, violent outbursts, make for a stark contrast to the Dude's declaration of being 'a pacifist' and genuine concern over Bunny's (seemingly) severed toe. This distinction is drawn out explicitly when Walter pulls his gun on Smokey during 'league' play over a disputed score. As the Dude notes, he was just a 'conscientious objector', who did not deserve to be bullied with such extreme aggression. Although Walter admits to having 'dabbled in pacifism' at some point in the past ('not in Nam, of course'), he clearly disregards the approach at that present time. After the Dude describes Smokey as having 'emotional problems, man', Walter cleverly retorts, 'besides the pacifism?' Still, despite their differences, both the Dude and Walter stand against the Nihilists from Germany. This raises the question, why do they disavow nihilism? And in favour of what beliefs? A potential understanding of this thorny situation can be brought about through a dual appreciation of the alternative, nonproductive masculinity discussed above and the film's political agenda, which is subtle yet ever-present.

While the masculine cult figure is entertaining and often comic in his presentation, he also offers a strong critique of larger themes that pervade the society from which he surfaces. Specific to the late 1990s, we find a prominent topic running through *Lebowski*: war. As discussed above, the Dude and Max portray alternatives to the conventionally masculine. However, we can also understand the Dude in conjunction with other cult males from the era and it is a testament to the Coen brothers that a single personality can be read to embody such a range of generic and character comparisons. In respect to thematic elements, *Lebowski* offers subtle yet poignant commentary upon the Iraq War (Operation Desert Storm), Vietnam, the Korean War and World War II, along with explicit questions about ethics and the value of human life. Similarly, a movie released just a few months after *Lebowski* revels in the anti-militant masculine: *Fear and Loathing in Las Vegas*. Set in 1972 (and closely following the trajectory of the original book), it takes place during a drug-fuelled romp through Las Vegas to cover a desert race, Hunter S. Thompson (aka Raoul Duke) and his attorney (Dr Gonzo) engage in an array of debaucheries while musing on the elusive 'American dream'. At the core of both films is the idea that things do not function as they should in America where too much deception, greed and power create a vicious 'square community' that ostracizes anyone outside of its control.

A steady stream of political terms flow from the Dude. Besides his claims to being a pacifist, there seems to be a persistent ideological tension percolating just below the surface of literal action. After being hit in the head with a coffee mug by the Malibu chief of police he curtly decries, 'Fucking fascist!' The world forces the Dude and the masculine cult figure to identify his political allegiance and typically that identification involves a critique or resistance of oppressive forces. The most common antithesis to the Dude is Walter. 'Say what you will about the tenets of National Socialism – at least it's an ethos.' One of the many memorable lines from Walter, it is also the rare apology for Nazism. Walter garners a type of cult following in his own right, but in the case of *Lebowski* he helps illustrate the Dude's perspective through contrast. The constant reminders of his veteran status, having seen friends 'dying face down in the muck', and ruminations on Operation Desert Storm as something less enthralling than Vietnam: 'Me and Charlie, eyeball to eyeball [...] the man in the black pajamas [...] a worthy fucking adversary,' as opposed to a 'bunch of fig eaters wearing towels on their heads' contribute to the reminders of a world at war. From the recorded speech of George H. W. Bush reprimanding Iraq's invasion of Kuwait to thugs tearing apart his apartment (and taking his rug), from Jackie Treehorn's control of the Malibu police department to the theft and destruction of the Dude's car, authoritarianism and violence loom large in a film often remembered as a lighthearted story about a 'lovable loser'. When the Dude confronts Mr Lebowski about being framed, he declares with great self-awareness that he was chosen as the mark because he is a 'loser, a deadbeat [...] somebody the square community won't give a shit about!' To which Mr Lebowski responds, 'Well, aren't 'cha?' The Dude acknowledges his distance from the mainstream values of society and it leaves the two of them at a stalemate. Each has shown his cards on the table, but there will be no reconciliation or change of heart, apologies or friendships. They are left at an impasse that neither language nor actions can cross. With that having been exposed, the Dude will inextricably reside on the margins and Mr Lebowski remains unchanged.

This need to stand outside of 'square culture', yet retain a belief in something other than 'nothing', drives the masculine cult figure and appears prominently at several points in *Fear and Loathing*. In a representative scene from *Fear and Loathing*, the duo of Duke and Gonzo realize that a conference on 'Narcotics and Dangerous Drugs' is taking place, drawing police personnel from across the country. They attend a presentation on the effects of marijuana by a Dr L. Ron Bumquist, who employs a vein of 'reefer madness' (chain-smoking cigarettes the entire time). Part of his presentation involves a classifications system of 'four distinct states of being' in order to understand what it is like 'inside the possessed mind': cool, groovy, hip and square. Side comments from Duke and Gonzo (who are casually sniffing bumps of cocaine) refer to the attendees

*Fig. 4: The Dude and the Narrator: A Texas-style cowboy and a 60s holdout, they prove a strange complement.*

and speaker as 'crazy', 'a nightmare' and 'fucking bullshit', alternatively. However, the structure of the talk and the desire to classify those 'freaks' and 'hippies' that smoke 'grass' presses up against the divide between middle-class values and the alternative masculine characters envisioned in these films. Post-war America craves organization, measured outcomes and planning. In many ways, these are the backbone of fascism, when taken to extremes. The masculine cult figure, however, resists classification as a figure and avoids performing such actions himself. He takes life as it comes, sometimes actively, often passively, yet always in a manner that avoids the stresses and pressures of square living. The ability to attain this existential position, to 'truly let the little things slide' as the narrator from *Fight Club* tells us of Tyler Durden; this is to live philosophically. *Fear and Loathing*'s Duke's famous 'high-water mark' soliloquy sums up what the masculine cult figure captures. Alone in a ransacked hotel room in Vegas, Duke explains how the mid-1960s in San Francisco were special because 'there was madness in any direction, at any hour, you could strike sparks anywhere'. Documentary news footage appears in black-and-white and grainy colour while he reflects upon the near past. Soldiers in Vietnam and college activists collide in the images, rolled together into a maelstrom of cultural unrest. The ephemeral, uncontrollable spirit of youth sent the message that guns and machines were not necessary to the revolution because 'our energy would simply prevail'. And perhaps most tellingly, 'whatever we were doing was *right*'. These characters live on intuition not intellect. Their decisions are made outside the bounds of rational philosophy and that *is* the philosophy. It is the unquantifiable aspects of life that drive these men and exactly why they pose a threat to the establishment. The countercultural parallels between the 1960s and the 1990s can be found in American history and film, too. The 1990s might even be said to serve as a light renaissance of the cultural revolution of the 1960s, wherein the rebellion is played out through individual, 'conscientious objectors' as opposed to mass protests. In one way, it may be alarming that the term 'pacifism' has become a punchline, but that may be the very point the Coen brothers hope to make.

In closing, I would like to connect one aesthetic point to the masculine cult figure, one that the films in which they exist share and constructs a significant postmodern theoretical frame. All of these films exploit tradition through their generic model. *Rushmore*, *Fear and Loathing*, *Fight Club* and *Lebowski* set their narratives within common, traditional genres, and then twist the conventions of that genre into warped reflections of their original natures. *Rushmore* is the academic *Bildungsroman* turned comic, *Fight Club* is the buddy movie turned violent, *Fear and Loathing* the road trip turned countercultural and *Lebowski* the detective story turned inside-out. In particular, the last two films mentioned reap large dividends from their inversions of standard genres. By turning the American road trip into a radical narcotics binge Gilliam (and Thompson) can ironically comment upon the romanticized nature of American culture in regards to the 'open road' while still using it to the advantage of the narrative. Likewise, *Lebowski* takes a similar (although I would argue more complex) turn in this respect. The Coen brothers essentially distort the classic private detective, film noir (and neo-noir) 'City of Angels' model of film-making (represented by canonized films like *The Maltese Falcon* [John Huston, 1941] and *Chinatown* [Roman Polanski, 1974]) and flip the premise. In comic, even absurd ways, the Dude gets pulled further and further into the middle of a detective story with plot twists, violence, suspicious characters and mysterious dames. However, his participation remains involuntary and an awareness of his status nonexistent. As the movie reaches its climax and passes through the denouement, this fact becomes ever more obvious. The 'real' P. I., Da Fino, admires the Dude's tradecraft and his being 'in bed with everybody', while the Dude seems unmindful of his own talents. But only a few minutes earlier, after having sex with Maude, the Dude had referred to his 'thinking about this *case*' as being all wrong, and realized that Mr Lebowski is the key to the entire saga. Whether consciously or not, the Dude has come to see himself as a 'brother shamus' on some level, he has taken to referring to the scenario that has been playing itself out as a 'case' in which we are to presume he is the detective. But this is not a usual case on any level. It devolves into (or maybe always is) a parody of a kidnapping case that makes the victim into a cause, detective into victim, and ransom into thin air. Even the language begins to border upon the nonsensical. The botched handoff turns out to switch a 'ringer for a ringer' and the victim 'never even kidnapped herself'. The reappropriation of noir devices for comic ends complements the masculine cult because it provides the ideal setting for subversion of standard expectations. As the Dude serves as counterpoint to Mr Lebowski in respect to middle-class masculinity and as political radical to the squares, his preferred genre is also anti-normative. If one feature can be said to define the masculine cult figure it might be that he pushes against the accepted standards, whatever they may be – cultural, thematic or aesthetic. ●

## GO FURTHER

### Film/Television

*Fight Club*, David Fincher, dir. (1999)

*Fear and Loathing in Las Vegas*, Terry Gilliam dir. (1998)

*Rushmore*, Wes Anderson, dir. (1998)

**'THERE'S JUST ONE THING, DUDE. DO YOU HAVE TO USE SO MANY CUSS WORDS?'**

**THE STRANGER**

# Fan Appreciation no.2
# Interview with Adam Bertocci:
# Author of *Two Gentlemen of Lebowski*

**Interview by Zachary Ingle**

**Zachary Ingle (ZI):** *Mashups mixing high-brow culture with contemporary popular culture have become popular in recent years. After the success of Seth Grahame-Smith's bestseller* Pride & Prejudice & Zombies (2009), *it seems like a slew of imitators followed in its wake. Were you inspired by some of these earlier mashups, or was* Two Gentlemen of Lebowski (2010) *something you had wanted to do for some time?*

**Adam Bertocci (AB):** This was sort of a whim. It began as a joke I posted on Facebook making fun of overly elaborate concepts. Only after the joke was made did I realize that, if executed properly, the Shakespeare-*Lebowski* concept might actually work – or at least be entertaining just for the sheer audacity of carrying it through. But it certainly wasn't something I wanted to do for some time – in fact, if I'd given the concept any thought beforehand, I might never have gone forward with it! I simply had a free weekend and a sudden yen to improvise in iambic pentameter. Hopefully the final product, even with the benefit of revision, still captures the joy of the impulsive rush behind its oddball genesis. I wasn't necessarily thinking of the classic-lit mashup books, but I totally understand the comparisons. I think the difference between those books and mine is, my book works better the more you know about the 'classic' source – this project is how close Shakespeare and *The Big Lebowski* are, not about how much Austen and zombies contrast.

**ZI:** *What was the origin of the play? Is it true you originally posted it online?*

**AB:** It was initially meant only as an elaborate Internet joke. I banged out a draft in a weekend, poked at it over the holidays and threw it online. The idea was to create a 'viral' calling card to get my screenwriting projects out there.

**ZI:** *Some of these mashups with classic literature fall into the trap of being too literal, but* Two Gentlemen of Lebowski *largely avoids this. How were you able to develop a new idiom rather than falling into this trap?*

**AB:** My process in the writing was simply to let the *Lebowski* content take care of itself, to trust it to survive in this new context. In a way, it's funnier if the reader has to take a little time figuring out what the translated line is – there's the 'aha' moment of discovery, however small, when your brain solves the puzzle, however simple. Just for fun, throw on the DVD of a movie you know well and pick a foreign language track, a language you might not have studied since your school days. I bet the reaction is the same. In any event, I'm guessing anyone who would want to read my book already has the movie memorized, so I felt it safe to assume certain prior knowledge.

I trace any success *Two Gentlemen of Lebowski* has had to the fact that the Dude and the Bard belong together, and complement each other – no shoehorning required. I could trust them to survive alongside each other, and amp up the Shakespearean language without any expense to *The Big Lebowski* at the core. When I was doing the revisions for the book, every effort was made to source each word back and either make sure it existed in Shakespeare's day or was close enough that the Bard might have realistically been able to coin it. (You can't do *Lebowski* without the word 'nihilist'. I tweaked the meaning a little bit to fit it into Elizabethan times. Thank heavens that marmots were already well-known.)

**ZI:** *Where has* Two Gentlemen of Lebowski *been performed?*

**AB:** I understand it's very popular at parties. Friends get together and pass the book around. There was one surprisingly worthwhile stage production. I say 'surprisingly' because I went in with no expectations and came out utterly delighted – I was expecting a bunch of second-rate comedians to put on costumes from the movie and treat the thing as an extended pop culture reference, and by some stroke of luck found myself among people who wanted to give the audience more than they bargained for. All credit goes to impresario Frank Cwiklik of DMTheatrics, backed by Horse Trade Theatre Group. It all goes to show that the universe has a mind of its own, sometimes to the better.

The world premiere was in March 2010 in New York, two months and change after the online version debuted. I was only involved as an observer; I know very little about stagecraft but was happy to watch and learn. Hearing actual Shakespearean actors deal with the dialogue, find the rhythms and all that, was incredibly helpful for me in revising the script for the book.

**ZI:** *When writing it, did you really think that it would be performed or just read in book form?*

**AB:** Well, I intended the initial joke to 'go viral', in the parlance of our time – and because I was crossing my fingers for it to become popular, I did say to myself, 'You know, if this becomes as popular as you want it to be, someone will want to perform it, probably in their college dorm basement or whatever.' So I tried to keep the stagecraft of it no more or less difficult than your average Shakespeare play – he was writing for the bare stage of the Globe and I had to think in the same mindset. But no, it's designed to be read, not performed – unlike Shakespeare, I hasten to add!

As for the book, having seen in New York what the project could be when people treat it with love, I was determined to make the book a special thing, not just a printout from the Internet with a few quickie corrections. At my editor's brilliant suggestion, it's designed to mirror the Shakespeare paperbacks you might have had in school.

**ZI:** *I especially like that you have footnotes, just as we are often accustomed when reading Shakespeare. Most are serious, but sometimes they contain some of the funniest material. The play also showcases your awareness of Shakespeare, as there are scattered Shakespearean quotes throughout (e.g. 'know the heat of a luxurious bed' [4.4.15], from* Much Ado About Nothing*). What is your academic background, particularly as it relates to the Bard?*

**AB:** I'm glad you liked the footnotes – I actually think they're the funniest part of the thing, but no one believes me!

As for the scattered quotes – the finalized script contains a quote from or reference to every single play in the Shakespearean canon. Plus a few of the side projects and bits of apocrypha. So happy hunting!

My academic credentials are nothing record-setting. I was a film major at Northwestern University with what I describe in my bio as 'a surprisingly useful minor in English literature'. I took three Shakespeare courses. In fact, the reason I did an English minor rather than major was that I didn't want to take a whole boatload of courses, I just liked Shakespeare! Well, Shakespeare and Oscar Wilde. Haven't found room for Wilde in a mashup yet, though. Pity, really.

I consider this project a labour of fandom, not of scholarship. Okay, some research was involved – but I'm no academic. Heck, there are even some things the Bard wrote that I've never looked at. I'm simply a fan with a sense of humour, and if my enthusiasm leaks through and convinces a few *Lebowski* achievers who suffered through Shakespeare in high school to give him another chance, I'll be awfully pleased.

**ZI:** *Your website mentions that you are also a film-maker and screenwrit-*

*er who used to make* Star Wars *fan films, among other things. What can you tell us about your other, non-*Lebowski *projects?*

**AB:** I've always loved fan projects. I got into film-making by seeing all the great *Star Wars* fan films being posted online in the late 1990s and thinking it all looked like fun. Among my better fan projects these days are 'Brooklyn Force', a *Star Wars* spoof about young hipsters fighting the Empire in their gentrifying neighbourhood ... 'The Chopped-Off Hands of *Star Wars*', which is Internet humour, self-explanatory ... and 'Overthinking Ghostbusters', the world's most absurdly complete analysis of my favourite movie ever.

I think that fan projects are a great way for people to sort of find their voice, see how the masters did things, learn the basics of telling a story on the page or stage or screen, crawl before walking. For instance, imitating Shakespeare has helped me in my own writing – I'm much more conscious now of rhythm, of how we pace our sentences and where we take a breath.

My personal work is painfully eclectic – as an example, right now I'm in post(-production) on a dramatic short about dancers, and this weekend I'm attending a screening of a comedy I did about the life and times of James K. Polk. I also write and edit other people's films. I wrote a children's movie starring Mickey Rooney called *Wreck the Halls* (David Abramson and Michelle Goetsch, 2008), and I've produced a few friends' feature films without actually putting up any money.

**ZI:** *How much of a* Lebowski *fan are you? Have you ever been to a Lebowski Fest?*

**AB:** I began this project as someone who enjoyed the movie and enjoyed studying it but didn't necessarily call himself 'a fan'. For me, being 'a fan' means being part of the scene. Enjoying is passive, fandom is active. To a certain extent, my distance gave me an advantage in writing the thing – I wasn't so attached to the film's words that it would have pained me to tamper with them. I came in with an outsider's perspective, which is something I haven't always been able to do with my fan projects – I mean, I've spoofed *Star Wars*, but it's so close to home, I've had no objectivity.

You can imagine that once this project came about, I got pulled into the fandom awfully quickly, and there's no zealot like a convert. I've attended three Lebowski Fests, hosted a screening, hung out in The Little Lebowski Shop in New York for more hours than I dare count, drank a few

Caucasians, met Julianne Moore, and, perhaps most absurdly, purchased one of the dancing girls' costumes from the film.

**ZI:** *Top bowling score?*

**AB:** Below a hundred, let's say that. Bowling is one of those things you can enjoy without actually being any good at it.

Chapter

6

# The Bard, The Knave and Sir Walter: Adapting a Modern Cult Movie into a Neo-Shakespearean Stage Play

Paul Rogalus

→ **American stage theatre today frequently recycles other forms of pop culture entertainment, such as films, old television shows, and pop or rock albums. This notion of recycled pop culture as material for Broadway and Off-Broadway plays hints at the financial importance for theatrical producers to find plays with built-in audiences, regardless of how shallow or unimaginative the 'work of art', much like film producers push for movie sequels and remakes.**

However, in the past six or seven years, an odd and somewhat contrary mini-trend has emerged, with popular modern cult films, such as Quentin Tarantino's *Pulp Fiction* (1994) and the Coen brothers' *The Big Lebowski*, being adapted for the stage using Shakespearean language. These cult neo-Shakespearean adaptations thus far have been staged in small theatres, for specialized audiences, which has allowed them to remain clever and imaginative, rather than simple, money-making shells.

Perhaps the first of these cult-film Shakespearean adaptations came from George Romero's 1968 cult movie, *Night of the Living Dead*. This low budget, but enduring zombie film was adapted by Brian MacInnis Smallwood into a Shakespearean stage comedy called *Twelfth Night of the Living Dead*, staged as a made-for-Halloween specialty production Off-Broadway in late October 2007. It has since been staged in a couple of other small theatres, but it is, as critic Kerry Lengel noted, a 'one-joke show'.

In 2009, a more ambitious cult film was adapted into a more ambitious Shakespearean-style stage play, when Quentin Tarantino's Oscar winning screenplay, *Pulp Fiction*, was adapted for the stage by Tedious Brief Productions, under the title *Bard Fiction*, by Ben Tallen, Aaron Greer and Brian Watson-Jones in collaboration with their 'Pulp Bard' wikispace. Their script for the play was very collaborative, and the original adaptors seemed to encourage changes and additions from participants and fans. The play was then altered and expanded by Her Majesty's Secret Players, and was re-titled *Pulp Shakespeare*. It has been staged numerous times in the past five years, and the original *Bard Fiction* was stretched into a two hour production and performed in Chicago in 2012.

*Bard Fiction*, and its many altered versions, uses Elizabethan language, while remaining very faithful to Tarantino's plot, tone and characterizations. The action of the stage play takes place in 1609, and the script itself is written as though it were 1614. In the play version, Tarantino's Butch character has become 'Sir Coolidge the Butcher, expert of the joust'; Marsellus and Mia Wallace are now Lord and Lady Wallace; and Yolanda (aka Honey Bunny) has been turned into 'Meadsweet Coney, a robber'. And Tarantino's famous pop culture wordplay on the McDonald's of Paris, France re-naming the Quarter Pounder with Cheese as 'Royale with Cheese', had to be transformed as well. Early on in the play, Vincent asks Julius: 'And know'st thou what the French name cottage pie?' The answer, according to Vincent, is 'Hachis Parmentier'.

Perhaps the most significant and most successful modern cult-film adaptation of this type was transformed into a Shakespearean stage play in 2009. Shortly after attending a production of *Twelfth Night* in New York starring Anne Hathaway, screenwriter and film-maker Adam Bertocci decided to adapt his favourite cult film, *The Big Lebowski*, into an Elizabethan-style stage play. He called it: *Two Gentlemen of Lebowski* (2010).

Bertocci notes in the Afterword to the Simon and Schuster publication of his play that he made the connection between *The Big Lebowski* and Shakespeare in part because of the timeless nature of the Dude, a lazy, White Russian-drinking misfit philos-

## The Bard, The Knave and Sir Walter: Adapting a Modern Cult Movie into a Neo-Shakespearean Stage Play

Paul Rogalus

*Fig. 1: Adam Bertocci's Two Gentlemen of Lebowski, in published form*

opher. As Bertocci writes: 'One can hardly think of Shakespeare's jovial, iconoclastic, dissolute genius Falstaff without wondering how he might enjoy White Russians or bowling.' Bertocci goes on to add that a second source of inspiration leading to his adaptation was his sense that Shakespeare loved a good penis joke. He saw the bawdy, lowbrow comedy of *The Big Lebowski* as a fitting vessel for Shakespeare's profane puns.

And so Bertocci turned the Coens' 'the Dude' into 'the Knave'; his bowling teammates became Sir Walter of Poland and Sir Donald of Greece; and the title character was adapted to Sir Geoffrey of Lebowski. The plot of Bertocci's play follows the Coens' screenplay faithfully, in plot and tone; as with *Bard Fiction*, only the language has been changed, transformed to that of the Elizabethan era. As with many Shakespearean comedies, the plot involves mistaken identity, in this case, the lowly Dude, or Knave, Geoffrey Lebowski being mistaken for a wealthy gentleman of the same name. The Knave argues against this case of mistaken identity in the opening scene: 'Thou err'st; no man calls me Lebowski. Hear rightly, man! - for thou has got the wrong man. I am the Knave, man; Knave in nature as in name.' He later qualifies this mistaken identity further, reworking a well-known scene from the film: 'I am the Knave, call'd the Knave. Or His Knaveness, or mayhap Knaver, or mayhap El Knaverino, in the manner of the Spaniard, if brevity be not in thy soul nor wit. A Knave by any other name would abide just as well.'

Bertocci's play has done extremely well, both in sales of its published script, and also in its productions. It has been staged in several cities, most notably in New York City, by the Horse Trader Theatre Group, to glowing reviews and very impressive box office numbers. For its premiere eleven-night run in New York City, which started showing on 18 March 2010, all eleven nights of Bertocci's play sold out by 25 January. During this time, Boston's Exquisite Corps theatre also sold out two nights of staged readings of *Two Gentlemen of Lebowski*.

In one review of the New York production, critic Marina Galperina notes the Shakespearean nature of the Coen brothers' film to begin with as leading to its success as a play: 'Familial tension, royal betrayal, and ill-fated dames and heroes grappling with morality are always a hit.'

So, it is clear that these recent neo-Shakespearean cult-movie adaptations have injected new excitement and life into the contemporary American theatre experience. The question is: why? What is it that's so special about these films, particularly *The Big Lebowski*, and what is it that makes them worthy of becoming Shakespearean?

Yes, Adam Bertocci has tapped into the already strong and rapidly growing *Lebowski* cult fan-base. He has made a number of book signing appearances at various Lebowski Fests. And Bertocci has also developed and maintained a *Two Gentlemen of Lebowski* Facebook page to help promote his play and keep it in the social media public eye. But there is more behind the ongoing success of this dramatic adaptation than clever and timely multimedia marketing, something more timeless and universal, something literary.

The Coen brothers and Tarantino are three of our great contemporary screenwriters.

Fig. 2: The DM Theatrics (of New York City) production of Two Gentlemen of Lebowski in 2010

They inject jarring violence into the middle of calm, quirky comic scenes, disrupting the pace and tone of audience expectation; they keep the audience off-balance to more thoroughly entertain them. Like Shakespeare, the Coens and Tarantino write tightly flowing, very clever, catchy and spontaneous dialogue, and most importantly, they create incredibly unique, idiosyncratic and memorable characters. Audiences don't just feel that they know these characters; they immerse themselves fanatically into these characters. Not only have these characters been portrayed in neo-Shakespearean plays, but they have also been the subjects of recent art exhibits. In 2011, the art exhibit entitled 'Quentin vs. Coen – An Art Show Tribute to the Films of Tarantino and the Brothers' opened, curated by Ken Harmon of the Spoke Art Gallery, featuring paintings, sculpture, prints and collage from over a hundred different artists from around the world. The art show had very successful exhibits in New York City, San Francisco and Los Angeles. Not only are these cult movies helping to revitalize American theatre, but they are generating a new sense of excitement into the American art scene as well. And once again, the cult hero characters are at the core of this artistic explosion.

The characters of *Pulp Fiction* and *The Big Lebowski* are timeless characters; they are characters who are worthy of being transported to the Elizabethan era. The cult fans of Vincent Vega, Jules Winfield, Walter Sobchak and the Dude recognize them as deep, universal and very real. They fit right in with the likes of Shakespearean characters like Falstaff, Prince Hal, Sir Toby Belch and Sir Andrew Aguecheek. The universality and humanity of these modern cult characters make them timeless inspirations for artists in various art forms.

But the cult fan-base of *The Big Lebowski* is unparalleled, eclipsing that of *Pulp Fiction* and every other film of our generation. And fans of *Lebowski* are also quite unique in their creative and scholarly responses and tributes to the film. Beyond Lebowski Fest, several tribute books have been published over the years since the film's release, celebrating the Coen brothers' movie in elaborate detail, such books as *I'm a Lebowski, You're a Lebowski* (2007), *The Dude Abides: The Gospel According to the Coen Brothers* (2009) and *The Abide Guide* (2011). Furthermore, there is now an actual religion in existence which is devoted to the teachings of the Dude, Dudeism, or the Church of the Latter-Day Dude; this church has over 150,000 freely ordained 'Dudeist Priests'. The spiritual nature of *Lebowski* has also led to the publication of such books as *The Dude De Ching* (2010), technically authored by 'The Church of the Latter-Day Dude', but translated by Peter Merel. And finally, in another classic literature connection, Phil Wells has published a book called *Dudesong* (2012), which reimagines *The Big Lebowski* in the style of a Homeric epic poem, predating even Adam Bertocci's period of literary homage.

The Coen brothers' central character, the Dude, aka the Knave, is as timeless and universal a character as we can find in literature of any age. As Bertocci sets him up in

**The Bard, The Knave and Sir Walter:**
**Adapting a Modern Cult Movie into a Neo-Shakespearean Stage Play**
Paul Rogalus

*Fig. 3 - 5: The DM Theatrics (of New York City) production of Two Gentlemen of Lebowski in 2010*

*Two Gentlemen*, he is 'A man of lazy ways, of epic sloth'. Above all, the Dude/Knave enjoys life, far too much so to be 'employ'd'. The Knave himself describes his character in Bertocci's play: 'I am but a travelling tumble-weed, and may well be carried by any wind, e'en south.'

In the film, the 'other Jeffrey Lebowski [...] The millionaire' calls him 'a bum'; in Bertocci's play version, Sir Geoffrey Lebowski calls the Knave 'a rogue'. He unleashes a critical verbal barrage upon the Knave:

> Indeed! "A pox upon't!" Tis thine answer to everything. Your merry revels have ended, sir. Let us condole the knight. The rogues lost; the rogues have always lost, will always lose, and so will it be tomorrow and tomorrow and tomorrow.

The Knave is a rascal, the fun-loving slacker buried deep inside most of us audience members. And since he is part of a play, rather than our own real-life encounters, we root for the rogue to win and to keep their merry revels continuing. And thus, we cheer when the Knave, upon departing from the critical Sir Geoffrey, lies and informs Lebowski's servant, Brandt: 'He bade me take away any rug in the house.'

The wealthy Sir Geoffrey, himself, vainly pontificating on the lazy lower classes as useless annoyances who disrupt and sully his world, fits nicely as a universal minor character, the sort of arrogant and self-serving aristocrat that Shakespeare so loved to mock, a sort of Shylock character, along with the sleazy trickster Jaques Treehorn, the timeless producer of pornographic entertainment, an individual who forsakes true art in order to make more money. Sir Donald works well as the Knave's Sir Andrew Aguecheek figure, a meek, cowardly buffoon and an ideal counterpart to the loud, aggressive, belligerent and very memorable Sir Walter.

With Bertocci's Shakespearean dialogue, the timelessness of Sir Walter's savage brashness becomes even more apparent and humorous, such as when he chastises bowling opponent Jack Smoke for breaking the rules by stepping over the line:

> Nay, I do protest, and draw my sword;
> It shall teach thee to disobey my word.
> Mark none but none into that bowler's frame,

> Else thou shalt enter into a world of pain.
> A world of pain, think upon't; unhappy world!

Sir Walter's explosive temper is even more clearly evident when he questions young Laurence Sellers regarding his involvement in the theft of Lebowski's ransom money:

> This befalleth when thou firk'st a stranger 'twixt the buttocks, Laurence! Understand'st thou? Dost thou attend me? Seest thou what happens, Laurence? Seest thou what happens, Laurence? Seest thou what happens, Laurence, when thou firk'st a stranger 'twixt the buttocks?

This larger than life, explosive, driven character has existed since the time of Shakespeare and his Sir Toby Belch.

Even the Coen brothers' use of a Greek chorus figure, the on-screen narrator of the film, the Stranger, indicates the epic and timeless literary potential of their script, as well as the generation-spanning nature of the Dude/Knave character, as the Stranger who narrates the film is himself from another era in America's past: the Old West, the wild American frontier. The Coens' narrator exists outside of the actual world of the film itself, serving to direct the focus of the audience onto the main character: 'Way out west there was this fella I wanna tell ya about. Goes by the name of Jeff Lebowski.' And in a sense, the narrator of the film mythologizes the Dude. 'Sometimes there's a man, sometimes, there's a man.' And Bertocci seized upon this chorus figure even more, providing the play with a Prologue and an Epilogue featuring the Chorus alone, as well as allowing the Chorus to interact with the Knave in a couple other scenes. The Chorus's ultimate purpose, in the play as well as the film, is to emphasize the timeless and universal nature of the central character: '"The Knave abideth". I dare not speak for thee, but this maketh me to be of good comfort; I deem it well that he be out there, the Knave, being of good case for we sinners.'

In Shakespeare's day, the bard had to appeal to the lower class as well as the nobility, in order to succeed in the business side of theatre, generating a broad and deep audience. Thus he mixed baser humour, through sexual innuendo and puns, with his classical plot structures and themes of mistaken identities and divided households, but in order to do so, he needed the most universal and human of characters. So too have the Coens and Tarantino blended shocking violence, dark humour and pop culture with classical plots and themes – through timeless, universal characters, eminently knowable and likeable characters – in order to appeal to the masses, both the filmgoing public at large, as well as the more sophisticated film students and scholars, the viewers looking for more. The Chorus for *Two Gentlemen of Lebowski* stresses this sense of characterization in introducing the Knave in the play's Prologue:

## The Bard, The Knave and Sir Walter: Adapting a Modern Cult Movie into a Neo-Shakespearean Stage Play

Paul Rogalus

The Knave, though scarcely a man of honor'd grace,
Nor god Olympian, nor yet employ'd,
Was nonetheless for all his time and place,
The man befits the circle he's enjoy'd.

Thus, even the Royal Shakespeare Company and the Folger Shakespeare Library showed appreciation for Bertocci's *Lebowski* adaptation, calling it 'Hysterical' and 'Laugh-out-loud funny'. The humour in *Two Gentlemen* is effective in that it hits the audience on multiple levels, from clever, character-driven wordplay to base bathroom comedy.

The American theatre has gone through a number of revivals over the years, primarily brought about by great playwrights who have given the audience captivating and memorable larger-than-life characters, such as Arthur Miller's Willy Loman, or Tennessee Williams's Stanley Kowalski and Blanche DuBois. In recent decades, however, these larger-than-life characters have been seen more in screenplays rather than stage plays, where the paychecks and audience size is much more considerable for writers, to the point of our most critically acclaimed and successful playwrights, such as Harold Pinter, Tom Stoppard and David Mamet, shifting to screenwriting.

The general filmgoing audience is broader in social and economic background, as well as being larger in number than the typical stage play audience. In recent years, the characters created by the Coen brothers and Tarantino, along with top screenwriters Charlie Kaufman, Paul Thomas Anderson, Kevin Smith, Martin McDonagh, and others have filled the void that has been created by the diminishing popularity of live theatre. The most effective screenwriting of recent decades, as far as characterization and captivating dialogue, has led to certain films developing cult followings, followings which have moved beyond the realm of cinema, for example, to the world of visual art and live theatre. And so, the cult success of the recent neo-Shakespearean stage adaptations of *Bard Fiction* and *Two Gentlemen of Lebowski* suggests that contemporary stage theatre in the twenty-first century is not dead; rather, it simply needs captivating, universal characters that a modern audience can know and love. Vincent, Lady Wallace, Sir Walter of Poland and the Knave *work* on stage. The audience knows them intimately, even more so seeing them live, in the flesh, human, vulnerable, onstage, speaking to us and speaking for us.

Thus when the Knave tells the Chorus at the end of Bertocci's play that he 'abideth', the Chorus says that this notion 'maketh me to be of good comfort'. Judging from the success of these play adaptations, it is reasonable to conclude that a great many of us do indeed take comfort in that. 'For never was a story of more glee / Than this of Geoffrey and the Big Lebowski.' ●

## GO FURTHER

### Books

*Dudesong*
Phil Wells
(Abide University Press, 2012)

*The Abide Guide: Living Like Lebowski*
Oliver Benjamin and Dwayne Eutsey
(Berkeley: Ulysses, 2011)

*Two Gentlemen of Lebowski: A Most Excellent Comedie and Tragic Romance*
Adam Bertocci
(New York: Simon and Schuster, 2010)

*The Dude De Ching: A Dudeist Interpretation of the Tao Te Ching*
The Church of the Latter-Day Dude
(Scotts Valley: CreateSpace, 2010)

*The Dude Abides: The Gospel According to the Coen Brothers*
Cathleen Falsani
(Grand Rapids, MI: Zondervan, 2009)

*I'm a Lebowski, You're a Lebowski: Life, the Big Lebowski, and What Have You*
Bill Green, Ben Peskoe, Will Russell and Scott Shuffitt
(New York: Bloomsbury, 2007)

### Extracts/Essays/Articles

'*Two Gentlemen of Lebowski*: A Tale of Nihilism, Ninepins and Goodly Rugs' by Marina Galperina
*Inside New York*,
Available at: http://insidenewyork.com/2010/03/29/two-gentlemen-of-lebowski-a-tale-of-nihilism-ninepins-and-goodly-rugs/

Chapter
7

# Reimagining and Commodifying Gender, Genre and Sexuality in *The Big Lebowski* for Cult Fan Consumption

Sheri Chinen Biesen

→ **I will investigate how Joel and Ethan Coen's 1998 film *The Big Lebowski*, its merchandizing strategies and virtual new media sites, reimagine and commodify gender, cinematic genres, and reframe sexuality to heighten appeal for consumption by fans as a cult classic. This fascinating experimental dark comedy spawned a remarkable array of loyal followers, fanatics and aficionados propagated in a thriving digital media realm of fansites, festivals and memorabilia.**

As the Coen brothers deftly drew on Raymond Chandler, hard-boiled detectives, film noir, Busby Berkeley musicals, singing cowboys and their own comedic neo-noir legacy in the wake of such films as *Miller's Crossing* (1990), *Barton Fink* (1991) and *Fargo* (1996), *The Big Lebowski* is itself all about fandom as a story told by a fan in noir-style flashback with voice-over narration, a visual feast of wit, spectacle and hilarity. This study examines *Lebowski* as a unique cinematic product and its cult fandom vis-à-vis gender, genre and sexuality, and how its appeal is maximized by virtual promotion sites, festival gear, posters, cast-and-crew photos, publicity, music, ancillary merchandizing, even custom-designed *Big Lebowski* toilet seats available for purchase to tantalize the hardcore cult fan.

Raised in Minnesota, which the Coens pay homage to in *Fargo*, Joel studied film at New York University and Ethan studied philosophy at Princeton before pursuing their film-making career with a series of stylish, offbeat independent films laced with their surreal, darkly comedic point of view. The Coen brothers invite 'fandom' in the movie *The Big Lebowski* itself. Written on the heels of their neo-noir films *Miller's Crossing* and *Barton Fink*, and set during that early-1990s period, *The Big Lebowski*'s postmodern genre experimentation encourages fandom and cult appeal. The 1940s film-noir universe of Philip Marlowe in Raymond Chandler's *The Big Sleep* (Howard Hawks, 1946) morphs into aging counter-culture hippie stoner the Dude in *The Big Lebowski* with pop culture references that proliferate in fan phenomena from websites to collectable memorabilia, fan merchandise and festival events.

Rather than a classic film-noir detective anti-hero remembering a flashback of his own lethal 'urban jungle' experience described in voice-over narration, in *The Big Lebowski* the role of the narrator is on the sidelines, a deep-voiced cowboy, the Stranger (Sam Elliott), who is a fan of the Dude (Jeff Bridges), telling the story. (The Coens recalled in a 2000 BBC documentary how Elliott asked them why he's in the film.)

The Stranger introduces fans to the iconic world of the Dude and Los Angeles in 1991. Elliott's folksy opening narration enhances the Dude's mythic legend as a fan narrative. The Stranger addresses the camera directly as a fan and invites viewers of the film to be fans and identify with a fellow fan in telling the tale of a 'stupefyin' character, story and setting. He admires the Dude's 'style'.

In 1998 interviews, the Coens admitted that *The Big Lebowski* is a noir homage based on hard-boiled writer Raymond Chandler-type stories in which the plot is less important. Rather, the detective moves from episode to episode, meeting unusual characters in an atmospheric milieu that captures the uncanny feel of Los Angeles (Dude's all-night Ralph's Market, dive apartment, driving and eating In-N-Out Burgers with a broken windshield as Santana's 'Oye Como Va' blares on the radio) to create a labyrinthine crime mystery-parody.

In fact, *The Big Lebowski*'s 1998 preview does not mention the story or what the film is about at all. Instead, it flashes a collage of images of crazy characters and scenes

**Reimagining and Commodifying Gender, Genre and Sexuality in *The Big Lebowski* for Cult Fan Consumption**
Sheri Chinen Biesen

with no description or narration. It features erotic images of pedophile sex offender 'the Jesus' (*Barton Fink*'s John Turturro) licking his purple bowling ball and shining it in his matching purple jumpsuit, despite his small amount of screen time in the film. The studio (Working Title/Polygram) may not have even known how to promote a film like *The Big Lebowski*, but it captures an alluring, fanatic cult fan-base. On the Lebowski Fest website, women fans emulate Turturro's Jesus: licking the bowling ball with abundant phallic innuendo, as in the film. (Jesus ball-shining T-shirts are available.)

As with other rabid fan bases such as Star Trek and Star Wars, fans of *The Big Lebowski* find iconic characters (the Dude, Spock, Yoda) and memorable, snappy dialogue ('Careful, man, there's a beverage here', 'Nobody fucks with the Jesus', 'Beam me up, Scotty', 'May the Force be with you') more appealing than the plot. Fans simulate *Lebowski*'s extraordinary writing, prefigured by the narrator in the film self-reflexively asking the Dude to curse less.

The role of the dialogue is key. At Lebowski festivals and promotion events, the fans create fan videos where rabid aficionados passionately shout out lines from the movie to the cast and crew at events, such as the 2011 cast reunion in New York to promote the Blu-ray release of the film. Devotees post their recorded home movies of Lebowski fan events on YouTube for other fans to enjoy, much like the Stranger sharing his tale as a fan of the Dude in the film itself. Lebowski sites post collectable fan images imitating the 'Last Supper' drawing, but instead of Jesus and his twelve disciples, the Dude sits at the centre surrounded by twelve characters from *The Big Lebowski* at a long table, with each person saying famous lines from the Coens' film. Numerous *Big Lebowski* Twitter accounts, such as 'Lebowskibot' aka 'The Dude' and 'Lebowskifest' stoke the flames of its cult status by quoting famous lines from the film and posting fan memorabilia, contests and events. On YouTube, BunnieLebowski posted *The Achievers: The Story of the Lebowski Fans* (Eddie Chung, 2009) documentary trailer as a video response with interviews from Bridges and fans, and described *Lebowski*'s growing fan phenomenon:

> First there was a movie from the Coen brothers called *The Big Lebowski*, then there was an explosion of the bizarre. What could have spawned a media frenzy over the course of 5 years, driving over 300,000 hits on the Lebowski Fest website alone and selling out over 17 events from Louisville to London giving birth to a sub culture correctly labeled as Achievers? What could gather such an eclectic crowd together relegating the best time one could have with a stranger in a bowling extravaganza?

Scott Timberg's article looks at *The Big Lebowski*'s cult following. He observes that, a decade after its release, *The Big Lebowski* has 'achieved cult status', and acknowledges the 1998 Coen brothers film as an 'undeniable pop-cult force: For many it is a way of life'. Festivals began appearing in Kentucky and elsewhere. Fans recited dialogue at a midnight screening at LA's New Beverly Cinema in 2000. Eddie Chung 'pondered' the 'mystery' of *Lebowski*'s 'resonance' after attending a 2004 Las Vegas Lebowski Fest event, a 'bout of bowling, trivia and White Russian consumption following the kind of screening in which audiences talk back to the screen' which 'drew nearly 1,000 people', inspiring him to make *The Achievers*, a documentary on *The Big Lebowski*'s 'cinematic subculture' where 'all of [his] nerdiest dreams come true'. Timberg suggests, 'Rather than collect perspectives from outside sources – film critics, scholars of subculture or fandom – *The Achievers* stays almost entirely with a core of die-hards.' He admits,

> It may make the film a bit insular but it also immerses the viewer in the world of Lebowski heads. Many of them – with their elaborate costumes, stressing out over movie trivia and fast bonds to other fest-goers – seem so obsessively single-minded it's hard not to wonder if they have much else going on in their lives.

In sociologically analysing Lebowski fans, Chung recalls, 'I went to a lot of their houses, and they had pretty healthy social networks. They let it out in the festival and then go back to their ordinary lives.' So what makes this Coen brothers film so popular for fans 'looking for first-rate casts falling into twisted pictures that create their own reality'?

The subsequent success of *The Big Lebowski*, and its emergence as a popular cult fan object, is remarkable given its tepid reception in 1998. Fans and the Coens admit it got mixed reviews and only spent six weeks in theatres. 'It didn't exactly bomb,' Timberg explains, Roger Ebert called it 'a genial, shambling comedy about a human train wreck' referring to the 'SoCal slacker played by Jeff Bridges'. Although *The Big Lebowski* has 'since been critically reevaluated and is now considered among the filmmakers' best, at the time, even Coen fans were puzzled by the movie's tossed-off plot and string of non sequiturs, and the film barely made back its budget'. Chung recalls seeing the film in Boise, Idaho in 1998. 'I was the only one in the theater.'

Adding verisimilitude as the Dude in *The Big Lebowski* (based on a friend of the Coens), Bridges interacts with the fans, performing at festival events, engaging with the film, its cast and crew, and behaving as a fan and fellow nerd on the set of the movie. Chronicling the production of the film, like a Lebowski fan, Bridges explained how he took pictures of the cast and crew, then made fan books to give to them. Exquisite images on the set of *Lebowski* include a deep-focus black-and-white widescreen shot of Turturro bowling, another of Bridges holding up the camera to take a fan photo of the Dude and the Stranger together admiring each other's 'style' at the bowling alley bar, and a picture of the cast and crew with Dude's car (wearing bowling pin headdresses which cast members kept as memorabilia) to remember the film experience in the spirit of a fan.

Like the film, its promotion perpetuates fandom. *Lebowski* fan/festival sites post cast/fan photos in costume. At fan events, cast members discuss their encounters with fans. They explain to fans in the audience that *Lebowski* devotees ('young guys') repeat-

**Reimagining and Commodifying Gender, Genre and Sexuality in *The Big Lebowski* for Cult Fan Consumption**
Sheri Chinen Biesen

edly stop them on the street to tell them it's their favourite film, which they've seen over and over, despite its initial lukewarm release. Like fans, actors described keeping costumes as collectors would. Bridges recalled using garments from his own wardrobe to play the Dude, but saved a bowling-pin hat as memento; Goodman kept his vest; and Turturro donated his purple jumpsuit to charity.

T-Bone Burnett's eclectic 'retro' music included different themes for each character: Bob Dylan, Creedence, Henry Mancini, Eagles and Gypsy Kings 'Hotel California' (Jesus's theme). Bridges showed up at a 2005 Los Angeles Lebowski Fest and played Dylan's 'The Man in Me' on his guitar, chanting 'a woman like you', the Dude's theme which opens the film, following the Stranger's theme, Bob Nolan's 'Tumbling Tumbleweeds' rolling from the desert across LA freeways. Fans interacted and performed with Bridges, recording and posting the event on YouTube.

As the Dude flies on his *Thief of Bagdad*-like magic carpet that 'tied the room together' and dances on Busby Berkeley musical dream-fantasy sets in the film, Bridges performs at the 2005 Lebowski Fest as female fans relish being pulled onstage with him from the audience and male fans relive the experience of wearing his jelly shoes and feeling the 'rush' and relaxed presence of the Dude. Hardcore fans and founders of the Lebowski Fest appear in fan videos. Fans enquire about Bridges's real-life similarities with the Dude character and compared the film to Francois Truffaut in a '*Cahiers du Cinéma* moment'. Fan sites like *The Dudespaper*, described as 'A Lifestyle Magazine for the Deeply Casual', even posted theoretical fan essays, as in California State University, Long Beach graduate student Lisa Donald's feminist analysis, 'Bowling, Gender and *The Big Lebowski*'.

*The Big Lebowski* emerges as a bizarre postmodern genre amalgam with multiple subjective stream-of-consciousness points of view and nightmare drug-hallucination fantasies and flashbacks that add to its cult appeal. So too, the narrative is structured around fandom and genre experimentation that reframes noir gender, masculinity and sexuality for cult fan consumption.

*Lebowski*'s opening Dude theme, Dylan's 'The Man in Me' with 'a woman like you' lyric, immediately suggests gender and masculinity. It reimagines male characters as anti-heroes in an absurd noir-style fan narrative which redefines classic tropes. The Stranger's voice-over narration begins the film by considering the nature of manhood in introducing the Dude: 'sometimes there's a man [...] he's the man for his time and place [...] possibly the laziest in Los Angeles county.' The wealthy Jeff Lebowski (David Huddleston) in Pasadena who shares his name later asks the Dude 'What is a man?' Fans posted a Cartoon Network parody of the scene between the millionaire Lebowski and the Dude exploring masculinity illuminated in amber tones as flames flicker before a crackling fireplace in the dark. Fan paraphernalia included photos of a life-size sculpture and video showcasing a handmade limited-edition replica of the Dude for discerning collectors. Like the film, these fan objects, sites and paraphernalia fetishize gender, masculinity and sexuality. Iconic textual signifiers are eroticized and exploited for cult fan consumption.

The entire film and its proliferation of fan phenomena revolve around the issue of gender, masculinity and sexuality. Just as the film parodies film noir with suggestive innuendo and sexual humour, characters in (and fans of) *The Big Lebowski* parody classic, recognizable noir-detective anti-heroes and femme fatales in terms of gender, sexuality and masculinity. Not only does the style, tone and existential spirit of *The Big Lebowski* draw on film noir; its themes play off of provocative noir issues of gender, masculinity and sexual identity.

The dark comedy deals with nymphomania, pornography, feminism and the Nihilists attacking the Dude's 'johnson'. Goodman referred to *The Big Lebowski* as a buddy movie, noting its male camaraderie. It can also be seen as a 'bromance'. Joel and Ethan Coen describe the relationship between Walter and the Dude as a 'dysfunctional married couple'. At the cast reunion in New York, fans posted videos as the vocal crowd of *Lebowski* devotees shouted lines of dialogue and trivia back and forth. Goodman described being a fan of the film: hanging out on the set on weekends during production, saving memorabilia and debating with cult fans in the audience about the nature of his male bonding relationship with Donny (Steve Buscemi). Buscemi expressed his reluctance ('I couldn't figure out why anyone would want to be this guy') as Donny, browbeaten by Walter, repeatedly told to shut up, and who eventually dies, his ashes hilariously scattered in the wind on the cliffs above the Pacific. When it was suggested during the press conference that Donny was possibly merely a figment of Walter's imagination reflecting his tormented masculine psyche, rabid fans in the audience shouted it was not true and insisted that Donny exists.

In reframing gender and sexuality, *The Big Lebowski* reimagines the noir femme fatale in Maude (Julianne Moore) and Bunny (Tara Reid). Maude and Bunny are outrageous, exaggerated parodies of the famous 'wild', 'bad girl' femme fatale sisters, murderous seductresses Carmen and Vivian Sternwood in Raymond Chandler's *The Big Sleep*, who are embroiled in a mysterious web of lies, blackmail, trouble, scandal and deceit. Julianne Moore, in particular, is a dazzling, liberated feminist rearticulation of a noir femme fatale as Maude. She is an independent woman who is comfortable with her sexuality and her gender infuses her creativity. Avant-garde feminist artist Maude affects a lofty accent, is strong, masculine, assertive, initiates and enjoys sex, paints nude and says fans/critics consider her work 'strongly vaginal'. She is proud of the sexual nature of her work and her feminist identity. Gold-digging, nymphomaniac, trophy wife and porn star Bunny offers sexual favours for money and mysteriously disappears while her misogynistic, nihilist porn co-stars demand ransom, and threaten and engage in violence. These active, sexual women are not romantic, sentimental or 'feminine'. Neither are they weak victims. They are in fact quite active in driving and propelling the very narrative of the film, which is all the more remarkable given the fact that it is often con-

**Reimagining and Commodifying Gender, Genre and Sexuality in *The Big Lebowski* for Cult Fan Consumption**
Sheri Chinen Biesen

sidered a masculine buddy movie. Like film noir, gender, masculinity and sexual identity also frame the narrative structure of the film and its elaborate flashback fantasy hallucination sequences which are in turn parodied in fan discourse and paraphernalia that exude *The Big Lebowski*'s noir styled issues of gender and sexuality.

Outlandish dream sequences ('Gutterballs') emphasize 'porn musical' sexual innuendo with phallic pins intersecting bowling balls and racy costumes that reappear in fansites and festivals. Intertextual homages abound. Fanart simulates femme fatales, Viking warrior women, 'special lady friends' and scantily attired dancers with bowling-ball bodices, pin headdresses and suggestive camera shots between their legs. The Dude flies beneath women's miniskirts through their spread limbs and relishes salacious sexual points of view evoking Berkeley's pre-Code Hollywood musicals which challenged censorship. The Coens explained computer compositing simulated Bridges's subjective point of view between dancers' legs and a motorized skateboard camera followed bowling balls striking pins.

The entire subjective 'erotic' point of view is thus driven by gender and sexuality. Posters for sale on the Lebowski Fest website include noir-inspired black-and-white images of a sexualized warrior femme Maude with her Viking helmet and bowling ball brassiere in a Chicago ad. An Orlando event featured a replica of the swimsuit-clad bathing beauty on the beach looking at the surf from *Barton Fink* with the horned Valkyrie helmet from *Lebowski*.

The popular Viking helmets in the film's surreal musical dream sequences suggest mythic Nordic Valkyries, legendary warrior women who take the spirits of dead Viking warriors to Valhalla, the heavenly place where spirit warriors spend their time feasting, drinking and fighting. It also conjures other pop culture references, mixing the aforementioned Berkeley musicals with iconography from the Warner Bros. cartoon *What's Opera, Doc?* (1957), itself an homage to Richard Wagner's classical composition 'The Ride of the Valkyries' from *The Ring* opera.

Tight women's T-shirts read 'Special Lady Friend'. Invoking Maude's naked harness painting in the film, a 'Strongly Vaginal' Art Competition was promoted by the Lebowski Fest website and Twitter and Facebook social networking pages. Publicity posters of dancers' spread legs and torsos adorned WHY Louisville storefront windows in preparation for the twelfth annual festival. Dude bobble heads sold out online.

Cult fans share posts, images, gifs, merchandise and videos that mythologize, fetishize, deconstruct, promote and celebrate fan events across social networks spawning a mass of devotees to the film and its festivals. The most impressive object of *Lebowski* fan phenomena was the painted toilet seat for sale with the multicoloured design of the Dude in long hair, sunglasses, T-shirt and sweater holding his half-and-half with the inscription: 'The Dude Takin' 'er easy for all us sinners' on the top seat cover. This opens to reveal the Jesus licking his purple bowling ball underneath, as well as cult fan objects (bowling ball, phallic bowling pin, Viking helmet, joint, Creedence cassette) and the caption 'This aggression will not stand, man', with the seat up to satisfy ardent *Lebowski* fanatics in search of their missing rug.

The swell of *Lebowski*'s thriving fan base of achievers and their cult attraction to the film is fascinating. Lebowski Fest co-founder Will Russell suggests, 'I think bowling has a lot to do with tying the fest together.' The film's 'brilliance' inspires fandom. 'It's an amazing, quotable movie that gets better every time you watch it. I've seen it over 100 times and I'll never get sick of it. I don't know how they did that.'

*The Big Lebowski*'s adroit use of dialogue and postmodern pop culture references catalysed its cult fan appeal. The Dude, Walter, Jesus and Donny's repartee are memorable and frequently quoted by fans at Lebowski fests. While other films use dialogue to serve the plot, *Lebowski*'s plot serves witty wordplay. Its absurd noir-flavoured black comedy, characters and stylish genre experimentation are unforgettable, adding immense appeal for hardcore fans. In his description of the Lebowski phenomenon, film critic David Edelstein notes, 'A cult gives its members license to feel superior to the rest of the universe, and so does a cult movie: it confers hipness on those who grok what the mainstream audience can't.' The Dude, the Stranger and a growing *Lebowski* fan base take comfort in the fact that 'The Dude abides'. ●

## GO FURTHER

### Extracts/Essays/Articles

'*The Achievers: The Story of the Lebowski Fans* explores The Dude phenomenon'
Scott Timberg
In *Los Angeles Times*. 30 July 2009, p. A-4.

'You're Entering a World of Lebowski'
David Edelstein
In *New York Times*, 8 August 2004, Available at: http://www.nytimes.com

### Film/Television

*The Achievers: The Story of the Lebowski Fans*, Eddie Chung, dir
(USA: K-Man Productions, 2009).

### Online

*The Dudespaper*, dudespaper.com
*Lebowski Fest*, www.lebowskifest.com

Chapter 8

# The Dude Goes Digital: *The Big Lebowski*, New Media and Participatory Culture

Peter C. Kunze

→ **One remarkable aspect of the afterlife of *The Big Lebowski* and its subsequent ascent to cult cinema status is the relative speed with which it achieved that level of subcultural recognition. Unlike *Reefer Madness* (aka *Tell Your Children* [Louis J. Gasnier, 1936]), which was reclaimed and re-appropriated, or *The Rocky Horror Picture Show* (Jim Sharman, 1975), which was especially embraced by a specific community, *The Big Lebowski* received mixed critical and commercial attention, but quickly rose to become a cult classic without clear demographic appeal.**

In her article on *The Big Lebowski* and replay culture, Barbara Klinger identifies the strong identification with the film for white males, though she admits this group, like any social demographic, has considerable diversity within it. Indeed, the fans are as varied as any film viewing population might be, and their enthusiasm for the film gives rise to a variety of fan practices. In this chapter, I survey the ways and manners in which *Lebowski* fans have embraced, manipulated and occupied digital spaces in order to share their love for this idiosyncratic masterpiece. By surveying fanfiction, YouTube videos and websites, I will show how the rise of the Internet, somewhat paralleled to *The Big Lebowski*'s own rise, has allowed for extensions on existing fan practices and the rapid development of new fields of interactions between viewers.

Despite its relative popularity in public discourse, 'new media' is an inclusive term that is ultimately fuzzy and flexible. Lev Manovich, in *The Language of New Media* (2001), explains that popular conceptions of new media imply 'the use of a computer for distribution and exhibition rather than production'. This definition is understandable, since computer usage in production is decades old, rendering 'new' useless. Manovich goes on to identify various defining aspects of new media objects, but for my purposes, numerical representation and variability are of primary concern. The use of digital code to compose new media objects renders media programmable, Manovich notes, thereby allowing people to customize the object rather than accepting one that has been produced and standardized for a wide consumer base. In addition, variability means that new media objects are infinite, rather than fixed, which allows for immediate reproduction and widespread dissemination of the object. The consumer now has the potential to interact and manipulate, creating the product he or she wants immediately. From websites that allow people to customize their digital profile to user-friendly software that permit home-video makers to edit their products quickly, we have entered an age of frequent appropriation and instant presentation. With freeware like IrfanView or commercial software like Adobe Photoshop, I can take a photograph off of the Internet, crop it, change the colours, superimpose text and create a new object that I can then post to Facebook, e-mail to friends and tweet. My authorship of this new text is concealed, and if I place my name on it, the next user can immediately remove it. With these capabilities in mind, nearly all self-expression and human interaction is subject to revision: Skype replaces phone calls, e-mails and texts replace letters, and a website replaces a resume and cover letter. Fan practices, therefore, are subject to innovation or, at least, transformation (depending on one's perspective regarding these digital technologies). Old practices become digitized, while new practices arise. Through a consideration of these various forms, one gets a stronger sense of how *The Big Lebowski* has fostered a unique fan community, how people who have never met nevertheless form bonds with complete strangers (sometimes anonymously) over a shared interest, and how digital technology may not, in fact, destroy interpersonal communication but rather reinvent it.

# The Dude Goes Digital: *The Big Lebowski*, New Media and Participatory Culture

Peter C. Kunze

The academic study of fandom builds upon work on reception and consumption, with early contributions by Janice Radway and Ien Ang. The seminal work remains Henry Jenkins's *Textual Poachers* (1992), in which Jenkins draws upon Michel de Certeau's theorization of poaching because it 'recognizes the power differential between the "landowners" and the "poachers"; yet it also acknowledges ways fans may resist legal constraints on their pleasure and challenge attempts to regulate the production and circulation of popular meanings'. While fans were ultimately subjected to the powerful interests of the corporatized culture that produced, distributed and exhibited their favourite texts, they nevertheless could interpret, appropriate and alter the texts as they saw fit. In this way, Jenkins ascribes his subjects a means of resistance as well as a useful way for understanding how such subjects display their agency. It is a limited success, though; Jenkins explains, 'Like other popular readers, fans lack direct access to the means of commercial cultural production and have only the most limited resources with which to influence entertainment industry's decisions.' Jenkins's subtle lamentation for fans against the victory of corporations is largely a reflection of his time (1992); now, some twenty years later, this power balance has significantly shifted to give the consumer more power (although, admittedly, not complete control). Jenkins acknowledges this trend in his 2006 book, *Convergence Culture*, where the fan from *Textual Poachers* has achieved a new level of power, agency and sophistication. The means of this considerable transition is not only the increasing role of digital technologies in our everyday lives, but the user-friendliness that makes it easy for users to compile their own CDs, edit movies, remix songs, doctor photographs and then widely distribute these (re) creations across the world. If the fan is the new hero, her weapon of choice is digital in nature. This chapter seeks to illustrate, albeit briefly, various strategies by which digital technology has empowered the consumer to create meaning but also to foster relationships with others, united only by their shared affection for the original text.

## Fanfiction

While fanfiction clearly is not a digital-specific genre, the use of the Internet to create, publish and respond to fanfiction fosters new opportunities for writers and readers alike. The ability to publish one's work immediately and receive relatively swift feedback from fellow fans allows writers of fanfiction to both assert their identities as fans of a source text and take ownership over the text itself. In her 2006 article, 'Fan fiction online: Engagement, critical response and affective play through writing', Angela Thomas identifies three strains of fanfiction. In the first, fans work within the world of the original text, using the characters and settings created within the source text. Crossovers comprise the second group, where worlds intersect, such as Star Trek and Star Wars, or Narnia and Middle Earth. The third, 'Alternative Universe' fiction, introduces new characters or settings into the original world, allowing for perhaps the most originality. Regardless of the strain the writer works within, fanfiction is an active genre with a thriving digital presence through sites like *FanFiction.net*.

*The Big Lebowski* certainly draws from surrealism, but it does not create the fantastic world one finds in the works of J. R. R. Tolkien, C. S. Lewis or J. K. Rowling. Perhaps for this reason *The Big Lebowski* has spawned a limited amount of fanfiction compared to other cultural phenomena like Buffy the Vampire Slayer or Harry Potter. 'The BIG Lebowski X Dragon Ball Z: The New Teammember' by Ian Menendez, combines *The Big Lebowski* with *Dragon Ball Z*: Goku, the protagonist of *Dragon Ball Z*, replaces the deceased Donny. The writer presumes his audience is unfamiliar with *The Big Lebowski*, so the story falters as he explains basic plot points in a concise, undeveloped manner. Trying to marry these two worlds proves difficult, especially since the reader would presumably enjoy two disparate texts: a postmodern film comedy from two highly regarded independent film auteurs and an animated Japanese series popular among schoolchildren. The most polished example on *FanFiction.net* is 'A Little Lebowski', written and posted by uncoveror. Five brief chapters in length, the story falls into the third strain Thomas identifies in that it proposes an imagined meeting between the Dude and a daughter he did not know he had with Maude, Artemisia. The Dude recounts the story told within the film itself, but uncoveror's narrative concludes with a present: a replacement rug 'that ties the room together'. While the story largely rehashes the film narrative itself, it also imagines a world beyond the film that nevertheless remains faithful to the spirit of the film. Furthermore, fanfiction allows fans to re-enter the world, especially if there are no plans for future instalments or prequels/sequels, and create such products for themselves. While some may deem these products derivative and unoriginal, these stories intend to build upon the source material rather than competing or outdoing it. Terms like 'derivative' and 'unoriginal' are misleading because they deny the graduated nature of art itself while privileging an outmoded concept of singular, isolated genius. Just as *The Big Lebowski* is the result of a collaboration between numerous professionals, many of whom are unknown by name or face to the fans that embrace the film so wholeheartedly, fanfiction, in its ways, enters the creative community that grew out of the original film production.

## YouTube

Since its launch, YouTube has proved to be an increasingly influential space for digital interaction. Celebrities have alternately used the site to talk to fans directly, release new or YouTube-specific content, and to 'vlog' (video blogging). Another key aspect to YouTube is the comments sections, where people can post their comments or (dis)agree with existing remarks. A distinctive use of this feature is 'trolling', where a user, behind the guise of an avatar, posts intentionally incendiary comments to anger a community or inspire a heated counter-response. Expectedly, these comments are often immature in nature, usually espousing racism, sexism or homophobia. Despite the potentially childish uses of the site, it also provides a worldwide forum for the

## The Dude Goes Digital: *The Big Lebowski*, New Media and Participatory Culture

Peter C. Kunze

Fig. 1: YouTube video "Donnie's Ashes"

exchange of videos, both existing and new, between users without requiring the viewer to download the content. This 'streaming' quality, in effect, allows greater traffic and viewing without risking the possible dangers of downloading.

Fans of *The Big Lebowski* have exercised YouTube and related non-online software in a variety of compelling ways. Since Windows MovieMaker and iMovie are standard features of computer software packages, the access to these technologies is easier than ever; Julie Levin Russo contends that this inclusion has 'facilitated an eruption of user-generated media'. The resulting products have found a home on YouTube (and similar video-sharing sites, like Vimeo and DailyMotion), where users can upload, stream and respond to video content. The most common articulation of fandom seems to be the posting of memorable moments from the film, which allows fans to replay without rewatching in its entirety. Considering YouTube's accessibility through a range of technologies, including smartphones and tablets, this method seems particularly useful based on the available time frame one has to work in. Popular scenes for rewatching include the introduction of the villainous Jesus (played by John Turturro) and the scattering of Donny's ashes. More creative means of fandom can be found in montages; in these instances, the user assembles images or movies clips in a manner that highlights key characters or moments and often replaces the original audio with a song from the film's soundtrack.

One particularly intriguing video clip, made by Hugh Sullivan Productions (YouTube ID: sullivan video) uses the dialogue of *The Big Lebowski* against visuals from *The Emperor's New Groove* (Mark Dindal, 2000). The result is an ironic contrast between the child-directed content of an animated film and the adult content one finds in *The Big Lebowski*. The Dude becomes Emperor Kuzco, Walter becomes Pacha (who was originally voiced by John Goodman) and Donny becomes Yzma. Though mildly successful in its execution and comic effect, the clip intriguingly ends with the production logo for Hugh Sullivan Productions. Admittedly, the basic materials were produced (and copyrighted) by other entities: Walt Disney Pictures for *The Emperor's New Groove*, and Polygram Filmed Entertainment and Working Title Films for *The Big Lebowski*. Yet Sullivan superimposes his name unto this new product, and this move is a key of fandom. Not only does Sullivan feel a right to manipulate these copyrighted, corporate-produced materials, but he then claims production credit over the new entity. This 'poaching' shows how fans and corporations wrestle over ownership – both within the text (in creating the narrative) and outside of the text (in interpreting and 'using' the final product, i.e. distribution and exhibition). While in 1992 Jenkins was concerned about the level of agency ascribed to fans, YouTube is indicative of the major shift digital technology allows the viewer. While not immediately producing wholly original content, viewers can easily capture, alter and disseminate their own creations that build upon their beloved source text.

Another form of poaching is the recreation video, wherein laypeople re-enact key

Fig. 2: Brandon Hardesty recreating scenes for YouTube viewers

scenes as a form of homage. As part of an ongoing series of movie re-enactments, Brandon Hardesty (YouTube ID: Brandon Hardesty) recreates the scene where Walter Sobchak (John Goodman) pulls out a gun in the bowling alley. Hardesty plays all of the parts, essentially acting with himself, and while the video is crudely shot, it does feature fairly accurate impressions of Steve Buscemi and John Goodman as Donny and Walter, respectively. The video has garnered over 200,000 views as of August 2013, and largely positive feedback in the form of likes and comments complimenting Hardesty's impressions. Despite better production values, '*The Big Lebowski* - Donnie's Ashes', posted by Tyson Rowley (YouTube ID: Tyson Rowley) as a school assignment, received considerably less favourable feedback from viewers online, with over four times more dislikes than likes, as of November 2013. Most of the comments devolve into purely uncritical trolling, but the contempt of more articulate commenters reveals a dislike of the video's tone, setting and acting. Unlike Hardesty's impassioned impressions, the actors in this video are markedly indifferent, which taints the original pacing necessary for the scene. Fans recognize this faltering, among other issues, and their critiques vary from frustration to fury. Though the quality of the technology and acting pales in comparison with the original, again these performances - much like cosplay at conventions - pay tribute while enabling the fan to enter the narrative world by becoming the character. Positive comments praise the ability to recapture the original as well as the fans' acting, the cinematic equivalent of the tribute band. Negative comments, however, reveal the community's intolerance of those who they feel diminish the film or fail to display the same level of commitment toward it. This policing of fan behaviour underscores a latent presumption that one can like a film in an improper or insufficient manner: fandom requires a certain unspoken level of enthusiasm and, when lacking, insults both the film and the fan community who has a vested interest in watching, discussing and celebrating it.

### Websites

The Internet Movie Database (IMDb) provides a variety of information about films, including the cast and production team, awards information and trivia. Users can even rate the film and interact with one another on the discussion board. As of July 2013, *The Big Lebowski*'s user rating is 8.2 out of 10 compared to the Metacritic rating of 69/100. This fact is unsurprising, considering cult cinema's tendency to buck aesthetic and narrative conventions in favour of subversion, trash, quirkiness or plain weird-for-weird's sake. As the name clearly implies, cult cinema finds its audience in subcultures, and, consequently, a direct challenge to mainstream sensibilities is characteristic of such cinema. Nevertheless, easily accessible, corporately-owned websites like the IMDb - owned by Amazon.com since 1998 - provide spaces that allow for the interaction and congregation of fans and interested parties alike. In her research on the film, Barbara Klinger uses the site's page for *The Big Lebowski* as evidence of the film's

**The Dude Goes Digital:**
***The Big Lebowski*, New Media and Participatory Culture**
Peter C. Kunze

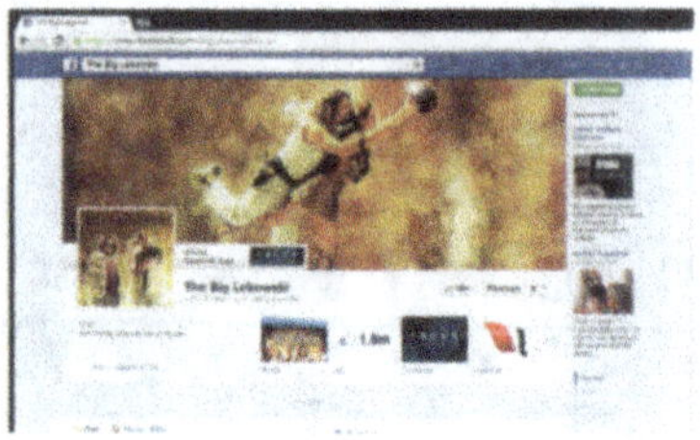

Fig. 3: *The Big Lebowski*'s Facebook page

ongoing international appeal. Perhaps the site's wide visibility, standardized design and corporate affiliation contribute to its success with users and its eligibility as a literal site for active, relatively safe and cordial socializing between fans.

In July 2013 the forum included 90 threads started since April 2013, and one thread initiated only two hours earlier had already elicited nine responses. Both in the number of responses and the level of activity, *The Big Lebowski* forum was more active than comparable cult film pages, such as *The Rocky Horror Picture Show*. The forum allows for various forms of interaction, ranging from a place for debating, polling, clarifying and interpreting. Debating seems to be one of the most productive ways to use these spaces, as fans discuss favourite characters or plot points. This discussion naturally folds into interpretation, and *The Big Lebowski*'s surrealist take on *The Big Sleep* (Howard Hawks, 1946) allows for various arguments. One recent conversation considered why Donny, who is regularly belittled by Walter, would socialize with the group. Some respondents speculated Donny was not real, based on DVD commentary, while others suggested Donny's ability as a bowler nurtured the friendship. The interaction veers into inside jokes, quotations and playful remarks, but the exchange allows fans to meet others who share their level of enthusiasm for the film. While conclusions are rarely met, the lively and playful discourse encourages a sense of belonging over common interests in a text whose open-ended, loose narrative counters mainstream Hollywood storytelling and, therefore, fails to garner popular acclaim.

Websites are the only genre discussed herein that are native to digital spaces exclusively, since fanfiction and videos predate the so-called 'digital revolution'. The website is a wholly new media object: it exists indefinitely yet not in one fixed location; it is easily manipulated by both creators and sometimes users; and its ultimate building block is the binary code. *The Big Lebowski* has spawned countless websites as well as webpages, like those on Facebook. The main page to 'like' *The Big Lebowski* on Facebook has over 1.75 million followers. It includes links to merchandise, information about cast members, film clips and photographs. The primary page that will appear in a search for fansites will be the official site for Lebowski Fest, a series of fests around the country that attract fans for movie-watching, drinking and bowling. In addition to maintaining Twitter, MySpace and Facebook accounts independent of their own site, *LebowskiFest.com* hosts a forum, a mailing list and photographs from past fests. The site's managers have streamlined the discussion into five sub-forums, where, according to site statistics as of August 2013, users have posted over 193,000 posts on over 4,300 topics.

A professional, well-maintained site, *LebowskiFest.com* legitimates Lebowski fandom in many ways by supervising and promoting various fests as well as encouraging other fan practices. Deeming fans 'Achievers', an allusion to the Little Lebowski Urban Achievers program, *LebowskiFest.com* also provides merchandise such as T-shirts, fest posters and bumper stickers. These items not only allow fans to participate in the fan culture through apparel and other visual signifiers of their fandom, but it also shows a developing industry around the film and fan culture-at-large. Action figures, clothing, festivals and conventions reveal the commercial potential posed by fan practices. In catering to these interests, both small groups like *LebowskiFest.com* and larger entities, like *CafePress.com*, which manufactures *Lebowski*-themed shirts, profit. What is interesting about the latter, and similar sites like *RedBubble*, is that they also predominantly make apparel customized by the users via the Internet. This level of creativity and interactivity speaks to the increased control the consumer (for our purposes, the typical fan) has in the marketplace as a result of digital technologies. The corporations may still possess a formidable amount of power, but the relationship between said corporation and their consumer has undergone a noticeable renegotiation in the digital age.

By occupying digital spaces and creating new media objects, fans have entered and engaged with new forms of agency to counteract the standardized mass production of corporate manufacturers. But while the advent of e-mail, smartphones and Facebook is often decried as a disease on interpersonal communication, the communities that have arisen around *The Big Lebowski* alone testify to the power of loving a text and of digital technologies to provide spaces and tools to share that love with others who have a similar passion. Not only can a 16-year-old girl in Alaska interact with a 40-year-old woman in Japan and an 80-year-old man in Miami instantly, they can forge a bond that may have otherwise been unavailable to them in their everyday life. Certainly such interactions can devolve into negative communication like trolling and cyber-bullying, but, at its best, new media affords fans further agency for expressing their enthusiasm and, by extension, themselves. The resulting products – fanfiction, viral videos, websites – testify not only to the power of narratives within our culture, but the power one gains and wields when one begins to embrace digital technologies to appropriate and contribute to that same narrative. ●

## GO FURTHER

### Books

*Convergence Culture: Where Old and New Media Collide*
Henry Jenkins
(New York University Press, 2006)

*The Language of New Media*
Lev Manovich
(Cambridge, MA: MIT Press, 2001)

*Textual Poachers: Television Fans and Participatory Culture*
Henry Jenkins
(New York: Routledge, 1992)

### Extracts/Essays/Articles

'The BIG Lebowski X Dragonball Z: The New Teammember' by Ian Menendez
At *FanFiction.net*, 2 June 2012
Available at: https://www.fanfiction.net/s/8174247/1/The-BIG-Lebowski-X-Dragon-Ball-Z-The-New-Teammemb

'A Little Lebowski' by uncoveror
At *FanFiction.net*, 17 September 2011
Available at: https://www.fanfiction.net/s/7384955/1/A-Little-Lebowski

'Becoming Cult: *The Big Lebowski*, Replay Culture and Male Fans'
Barbara Klinger
In *Screen* 51: 1 (2010), pp. 1-20.

'User-Penetrated Content: Fan Video in the Age of Convergence'
Julie Levin Russo
In *Cinema Journal* 48:4 (2009), pp. 125-130.

'Fan fiction online: Engagement, critical response and affective play through writing'
Angela Thomas
In *Australian Journal of Language and Literacy* 29:3 (2006), pp. 226-239.

**Online**

'The Dude's New Groove' [YouTube], 22 September 2012, www.youtube.com/watch?v=trKTHFJfTVU

'*The Big Lebowski* - Donnie's Ashes' [YouTube], 15 November 2007, www.youtube.com/watch?v=ulkLccua9TQ

'Reenactment #14: *The Big Lebowski*' [YouTube], 4 August 2006, www.youtube.com/watch?v=ml-PxIRWhRo

*Lebowski Fest*, www.lebowskifest.com

# Fan Appreciation no.3
# Interview with Kim Barber: Executive Producer of *The Achievers* (2009)

**Interview by Jeremy Hehl**

**Jeremy Hehl (JH):** *What was it that first inspired you to produce a documentary about these Lebowski Fests? Were you a diehard fan of* The Big Lebowski *prior to filming the doc?*

**Kim Barber (KB):** [Director] Eddie [Chung] was a friend of an acquaintance of mine. I was at a social event with said acquaintance, who incidentally, had also been involved with the *Achievers* project with Eddie. We asked him for a status update and he told us he had run out of money. So we decided to invest in the project and help Eddie move into the final stages of production and filming.

**JH:** *Eddie was in the research phases to platform the film, and was going to festivals and events looking for investors?*

**KB:** He had been filming for seven years. He dedicated a couple of years to the film; I don't think he was even working – well he was, but you know what I mean...he would go to various festivals and garner support for his project, and he eventually found me. He even stayed at my house for a few weeks.

**JH:** *How did Eddie first approach you with the idea about the film? Are you a* Lebowski *fan?*

**KB:** We met at the festival, went to a few Lebowski Fests, became friends and then partners in the film. I have been a *Lebowski* fan for years. At first I thought the festivals weird – these people sit there in costume and quote the film. The forums were pretty hot and heavy, and created a lot of relationships. Those core forum members were the source for Eddie's film. It's inarguably a cult following. There was a race to do the documentary, but Eddie had the longest running relationship with Will and Scott and was the clear frontrunner to make the documentary about Lebowski Fest.

**JH:** *How would you explain your relationship with Will Russell and Scott Shuffitt?*

**KB:** Um, I have a good relationship with Will and Scott. We went to some festivals, and 'press-passed' several events. They are in our movie and by the time I got involved with the film, Eddie had already secured the rights with Universal Studios to be the exclusive documentary allowed to use footage from Lebowski Fest in a film. You know Scott and Will wrote a book about *Lebowski*, and so they helped us really understand who the Achievers actually are. The last I've heard, Scott is no longer working with the Fests while Will has remained and continues to organize these events. I could pick up the phone and talk to them at any moment, I would consider them...

**JH:**...*like Walter and Donny?*

**KB:** Yeah, friends.

**JH:** *Do you think the delivery of the documentary turned out as Eddie planned? In your opinion, what was the intended message of the film?*

**KB:** Well, there were two versions of the movie: one, the first version, we watched in Louisville at a Lebowski Fest, and then there is the version which has been released to the public on Netflix. The executive producers liked the first version more – the one we saw in Louisville, but the second is the one Eddie liked, and he wanted to have his artistic input only. I think the ending of the film Eddie released caused a bit of a stir with Will and Scott because it insinuated that Lebowski Fest could fade away. It didn't fade away as fast as Eddie anticipated – even though the core of the Lebowski Fest, at least according to our film, the forums, have gone dormant over these past five or six years. Life cycles, you know? Eddie wanted to show how this film affects people in their day-to-day lives. He was looking for the really human story in all of this, and I think he got it.

**JH:** *Given that* The Big Lebowski *has become a wildly popular cult film, and now that* The Achievers *is adding to that mystique, do you believe that Lebowski Fest will continue to attract more Achievers?*

**KB:** Yes. I've been invited to festivals all over Europe and the US. I think the film will continue to grow in popularity. I don't want to speak for him directly, but I would be curious to see if Will wants to continue running the festivals. Organizing these events is a lot of work, and for a while sponsors were coming in and doing mini-fests, which weren't as successful, but the main Lebowski Fest continues to grow and attract Achievers....There may be a possibility that the events will run their course....I would be surprised if they are still going on in twenty years.

**JH:** *Do you believe* The Achievers *has created a sense of 'the weird' for* *potential future fans of* The Big Lebowski? *Does the film intentionally or unintentionally showcase the strange aspects of* Lebowski *fandom?*

**KB:** I don't know if I would use the word strange. It's certainly an interesting bond these fans have about this movie. I walk into crowds of people small and large and there is always someone who loves this movie.

**JH:** *What about the Walrus, Kim?*

**KB:** Haha, Stormy? Her passion for this film is interesting to watch. She too has moved away from it, and I don't know what she is doing these days.

**JH:** *How did Eddie decide who to interview and which segments of the footage to include in the film? How much footage of these events do you have in total? Did you make executive decisions in post[-production]?*

**KB:** Eddie made it very clear it was his decision, and quite honestly I'm not a filmmaker, so that was fine for me. We hired a creative team for his use. Eddie followed the core of the *Lebowski* fandom phenomena through the Lebowski Fest forums. He wanted to tell their story, and through them he surreptitiously told the story of all the Achievers. The people you see in the movie are those who had the strongest ties on the forums. Eddie was intimately involved in the forums.

**JH:** *Was there any resistance from any of the Achievers? Were there any of these individuals who created headaches for you during the process? Any production issues?*

**KB:** No, everyone was very supportive of getting a film out there.

**JH:** *Was it difficult to get your foot in the door with Jeff Bridges and the other cast members?*

**KB:** No. All of the cast members were extremely supportive, signed the releases and wished us luck, but the music was a different story.

**JH:** *What is the central binding ideology of the Achievers from your experiences? Do you abide by the same philosophies?*

**KB:** It has become a religion. I've been around the diehards. People who quote the film in every other sentence. I think it's the nature of the Dude that draws people in. He's normal. It left me speechless when I went to Chicago and there was 1200 people sitting in a theater quoting this movie in perfect unison. It's as simple as a t-shirt that says 'the Dude abides.' Friends for life.

**JH:** *What is your hope for the future of* The Achievers? *What do you hope the film accomplishes...in the long run?*

**KB:** From an executive producer role, there has not been as many sales as my investment would have liked. That's the most appropriate way to say it. Eddie is a one-man show. In hindsight, the marketing and development of the film could have been more elaborate.

**JH:** *In terms of distribution, how has the film done, and what do you anticipate for* The Achievers *in the future?*

**KB:** It's on Netflix, but we want more.

**JH:** *Did you make a profit off of the film?*

**KB:** No.

**JH:** *Well, have you learned to take it easy, Kim?*

**KB:** Absolutely. Is that a line from the film?

# 'SMOKEY, THIS BE NOT THE FOUL JUNGLES OF THE DARKEST EAST ORIENT. THIS BE NINEPINS. WE ARE BOUND BY LAWS.'

**WALTER**
TWO GENTLEMEN OF LEBOWSKI

Chapter
9

# Listening Deeply to *Lebowski*: One Fan's Attempt to Draw a Musical Map Surrounding the Dude

Tom Zlabinger

→ **Music's role in the construction of the world in the Coen brothers' 1998 cult classic *The Big Lebowski* not only sets the mood, but also helps define the identity of many of the main characters in the film. As a fan, I love how music propels the story, including two choreographed dream sequences without dialogue. But when I purchased and seriously listened to the soundtrack on CD, I was surprised by the diversity of the music in the film, but disappointed that the soundtrack did not contain more of the most dramatically and historically important music in the film, like Creedence Clearwater Revival.**

I hope that deep listening to all the film's music and an examination of its use will provide a critical exploration to help other fans enjoy and dig deeper into the Lebowski world.

I hoped originally to examine what fans of *The Big Lebowski* thought of the music and its use and assembled a brief survey to learn from fans about how the film's music informed their understanding of the movie and the construction of characters' identities. But after meeting and e-mailing several fans, I quickly realized that the film's music was not of much interest to them. They knew the music, but were not eager to discuss it, or provided short answers that were not revealing. In her 2009 essay 'Holding Out Hope for the Creedence: Music and the Search for the Real Thing in *The Big Lebowski*', Diane Pecknold related similar findings: 'fans seem to have found music itself to be inadequate to the task of recreating or communicating the mood of the film.' But I insist the music of the movie is worth examining. Pecknold has already written about issues of authenticity and the use of music in the film. Instead of looking at how a group of fans of the film think and feel about the music, I am hoping that as an obsessed fan myself, I can create a musical map of the Lebowski world and provide a discussion that would then in turn be of benefit and interest to other fans.

*The Big Lebowski* was the first film by the Coen brothers to use pre-existing music. Their previous seven films all had original soundtracks composed for each film. But aside from a few cues by composer Carter Burwell, the music of *The Big Lebowski* is mostly 'source' music, recordings that had a life before the film, so their own historical and cultural context informs the Lebowski world. Ethan Coen spoke of conceiving the look and feel of the film in *The Big Lebowski: The Making of a Coen Brothers Film* (1998), stating that he wanted 'no lava lamps or that kind of shit. No Day-Glo posters on the wall of [the Dude's] house. No Grateful Dead music on the soundtrack'. To help create this feel, the Coen brothers asked Bob Dylan band alumnus T-Bone Burnett to help select music and was dubbed 'music archivist' for the film. In a *New York Times* article, Joel Coen stated, 'We knew we wanted different genres and music from different times. Creedence to Nina Simone to Moondog to Dylan. T-Bone even came up with some far-out Henry Mancini and Yma Sumac.' Given that the Coens and Burnett were avoiding bands like the Grateful Dead and being adventurous in choosing music from different genres, how does this resulting sonic world inform the film and its characters?

In order to create a more complete vision of the music found in the Lebowski world, I have organized the music from the entire movie into a map (see table below) and have grouped the music into three levels: music the Dude chooses, music the Dude does not choose, and non-diegetic music (sound that has no visible source in the film) that the Dude may or may not hear.

## Music the Dude chooses

The Dude chooses music several times on his stereo, on his Walkman or in his car. First, he is seen listening to Captain Beefheart's 'Her Eyes are a Blue Million Miles' (1972) while checking the messages on his answering machine. In the song, Beefheart sings of someone who does not understand why he is loved by another woman: 'I look at her and she looks at me / In her eyes I see the sea / I don't see what she sees in a man like me / She says she loves me.' Later, we see the Dude listen to Bob Dylan's 'The Man in Me' (1970) during the first dream sequence and as he wakes up from it. Within the song, Dylan further elaborates the divide between a man and a woman, revealing a man's insecurity: 'The man in me will hide sometimes to keep from being seen / But that's just because he doesn't want to turn into some machine / Take a woman like you / To get through to the man in me.' These two ideas together create an idea of love between a man and a woman that is full of insecurity, but also the hope of being liberated and thus avoiding the fate of turning 'into some machine'.

The Dude is also a Nina Simone fan. Post-coitus, he and Maude listen to Simone sing Duke Ellington's classic 'I've Got it Bad (and that Ain't Good)' (1962). Similar to the themes of the Beefheart and Dylan tunes, Simone sings of a love out of balance: 'Lord above me make him love me the way he should / I've got it so bad and that ain't good.' If the voices of Beefheart, Dylan and Simone are heard together, we begin to understand that the Dude is a man who is at least in love with the process of love, though he may not be that successful when it comes to women. In her article, Pecknold points out:

> nearly all of the music The Dude listens to is united by an obsession with romantic longing [...] The Dude surrounds himself not with the culturally and socially politicized music with which his favorite artists (and the hippie counter-culture he theoretically represents) are most commonly associated, but with the expressions of desire for elusive or mysterious love.

The Dude is a romantic, and his tastes are more sophisticated than one might think at first.

In addition to his romantic side, the Dude loves music that has a good beat. The Dude avidly listens to Creedence Clearwater Revival in his car. (Luckily, he got his tapes back after his car was stolen!) The Dude also bops his head to music like Elvis Costello's 'My Mood Swings' (1998), which he listens to on his Walkman while at the doctor. And though it may be on the radio rather than his tape player, we can see the Dude enjoying the Latin rhythms of Santana's 'Oye Como Va' (1970), the music blasting out the windows of his car as he, Walter and Donny eat on the way home from In-N-Out Burger. This mixture of romance and dance rhythms shows a side of the Dude that is more than just a burned-out hippie who might like psychedelic music. According to *The Big Lebowski Wiki*, the Dude was born in 1942. He would have been in high school and college before music became psychedelic in the mid-1960s, which makes sense if he worked on the original draft of the Port Huron Statement before it was published in 1962. We can therefore infer that his musical tastes would probably have been influenced more by jazz and R&B of the 1950s than by 1960s psychedelia.

Also, the Dude listens to soundscapes to help him relax. Before Maude reclaims her stolen rug, the Dude listens to a self-made tape entitled 'Venice Beach League Playoffs'; simply the sounds of bowling balls rolling down lanes and knocking down pins. Later, while taking a bath, he is listening to *Song of the Whale: Ultimate Relaxation*.

Finally, we must not ignore the moment when the Dude sings! While drugged by Jackie Treehorn and on the way to the police station in the back of a cop car, we hear the Dude sing words from the theme song to the mid-1960s TV western series *Branded* (Larry Cohen, NBC, 1965-1966): 'He was innocent / Not a charge was true / And they say he ran away / Branded!' Though the lines of the song are slightly out of order the theme song is worth noting, as the TV series was about a man falsely accused of desertion. Does the Dude see himself as someone who was falsely accused or as someone who has abandoned the cause? Or is this just another flashback? Whatever the reason, the final lines of the song (which the Dude does not sing in the movie) are telling: 'What do you do when you're branded, and you know you're a man? / Wherever you go for the rest of your life you must prove [...] you're a man.' Proving oneself dovetails nicely with the theme of unbalanced love in the lyrics of Beefheart, Dylan and Simone. How do you prove you are a man if you are not successful in your love life? Given that the Dude has no definitive career goals, some of the answer can be found when Maude asks him what he does for recreation. 'Oh, the usual. I bowl. Drive around. The occasional acid flashback.' The Dude is happy being a loner. But the music he chooses to listen to and sing tells a different, even more openended story. Pecknold is right that the Dude is obsessed with romantic longing, but this fragment from *Branded* tweaks the situation and provides a little more depth to the Dude. He is not only longing for love, but also longing for manhood. He may also simply enjoy the search, which would be most Dude-like, but looking at all of the music he chooses, we see the Dude may be looking for more than just love.

## Music the Dude does not choose

The music the Dude does not choose is a wider array. The Dude hears music at the bowling alley, while visiting Mr Lebowski and Maude, and in other situations. The first music he hears (and the first diegetic music and a tune repeated throughout the movie) is Dylan's 'Man in Me' at the bowling alley, when we meet Walter and Donny for the first time while the Dude explains what happened to his rug. Other songs the Dude hears in the bowling alley are The Monks's 'I Hate You' (1966), Booker T & the M.G.'s' 'Behave Yourself' (1962), Elvis Costello's 'My Mood Swings', the Sons of the Pioneers's 'Tumbling Tumbleweeds' (1946) and Townes Van Zandt's 1993 cover of the Rolling Stones's 'Dead Flowers'. We can assume that these are songs either on the radio or on the jukebox at the bowling alley. (But given the tunes heard, these are probably singles on a jukebox rather than music on the radio.) The music in the bowling alley is not too different from what the Dude chooses elsewhere. This is not a surprise, as the bowling alley is obviously the Dude's home away from home.

Other music the Dude encounters is in strong contrast to what the Dude chooses to listen to and what he hears in the blowing alley. We see Mr Lebowski listening to classical music (Mozart's *Requiem* and Korngold's *Die tote Stadt/The Dead City*) the first two times the Dude visits him regarding Bunny's abduction, creating a mood of sorrow. And the Dude's landlord uses classical music ('The Gnome' from Mussorgsky's *Pictures at an Exhibition*) during the dance piece the Dude sees. The contrast of classical music separates Mr Lebowski's residence and the landlord's dance piece as places outside the Dude's usual surroundings.

The Dude is subjected to even more contrasting pieces during the movie. He hears Latin-inspired lounge music when he meets Bunny for the first time (Esquivel's 'Mucha Muchacha' [1962]) and when he visits Jackie Treehorn (Henry Mancini's 'Lujon' [1959]). He also hears overly stylized music booming out of Bunny's convertible (Big Johnson's cover of Elvis Presley's 'Viva Las Vegas') and when he is ejected from a cab after expressing his opinion of a certain classic rock band (The Eagles's 'Peaceful Easy Feeling' [1972]). Both songs are overtly mainstream and have nothing to do with finding true love. In fact, both are the opposite of the Dude's longing for love. 'Viva Las Vegas' is in praise of excess and love of dominating women: 'There's a thousand pretty women waiting out there / And they're all livin' devil may care / And I'm just the devil with love to spare.' And the Eagles's 'Peaceful Easy Feeling' is void of any mystery of love and its longing as the singer has found love. The messages of both these songs are not very Dude-like. When we remember that the Dude is happiest bowling, driving and flashing back, excess and actually finding love are not compatible to what the Dude truly values and experiences.

While visiting Maude, the Dude hears not only the funky soundtrack to the porno film 'Logjammin' (Piero Piccioni's 'Traffic Boom' [1974]), but also the ethereal sounds of Russian chant (Rustavi Folk Choir's 'We Venerate Thy Cross'). Pecknold has already done a marvelous job discussing the music found in Maude's record collection. Though the Dude does not hear this music, it is interesting that he does not comment on nor react to the music he finds in her collection while looking for the Autobahn album. The music heard while visiting Maude is almost the furthest from the Dude's musical preference.

But one could argue that the most contrasting piece the Dude hears is Autobahn's 'Technopop' (Carter Burwell, 1998) played on a boom box after the Nihilists (who are all three members of Autobahn) have set the Dude's car on fire. With synthesizers, robotic voices and the lyrics, 'We believe in nothing / Wir glauben an nichts,' we have come dangerously close to Dylan's fear of turning 'into some machine'. In fact, when we see the cover of Autobahn's album *Nagelbett/Bed of Nails*, the artwork is a near copy of the cover of *Die Mensch-Maschine/The Man-Machine* (1978) by Germany's electronic music pioneers Kraftwerk, even down to the red shirts and black ties. The scene is easily the climax of the entire film with the final destruction of the Dude's car, the altercation with the Nihilists and the death of Donny. So it is only fitting that the most contrasting or distant music the Dude hears is at the most climactic moment of the film.

If the music not chosen but heard by the Dude is viewed as a whole, we instantly see a layer of otherness surrounding the Dude sonically. The bowling alley is an extension of who he is. Therefore, the music is quite compatible to what he already chooses. But when the Dude is with Mr Lebowski, Bunny, Maude, Jackie Treehorn or the Nihilists, the music is arguably the most different and contrasting to the innermost layer of the Dude's world.

### Non-diegetic music

Finally, the outermost layer of music in the Lebowski world has an even higher contrast to the Dude's musical preference. The opening of the film uses 'Tumbling Tumbleweeds' by the Sons of the Pioneers. The group originally featured 1940s and 1950s cowboy icon Roy Rogers, perhaps nostalgic for the Dude as part of his childhood. But given the nondiegetic use of the tune (except when he may have heard the Muzak version while writing a $.69 check for half-and-half), we cannot assume that the Dude hears the tune. It is only a part of the larger musical landscape of the film as perceived by the viewer. 'Tumbling Tumbleweeds' crosses over into the diegetic layer when the Dude could hear it in the bowling alley while speaking with the Stranger for the first time. But the use of the tune non-diegetically is so strong that we must see and hear it positioned firmly in this outer layer.

In addition to 'Tumbling Tumbleweeds', other music contrasts to the Dude's musical preference: The Chieftains's cover of 'Hotel California', Peruvian singer Yma Sumac's exotic vocals in 'Ataypura' (1950), Kenny Rogers's 'Just Dropped In (To See What Condition My Condition Was In)' (1968), Moondog's ominous classical piece 'Stamping Ground' (1970) and finally Shawn Colvin's down-tempo cover of 'Viva Las Vegas'. This collection of music looks very eclectic on the surface. But the use of the music in the non-diegetic layer gives the repertoire a cohesion in its otherness. Coupled with 'Tumbling Tumbleweeds', this music is very cinematic and otherworldly, playing with multiple ideas of convention. After the nostalgia of 'Tumbling Tumbleweeds', the Chieftains's Eagles cover sounds very exotic with its flamenco rhythms and Spanish lyrics. And Sumac's sounds and four-octave range only furthers this exoticism. Although the Coen brothers and Burnett had hoped to avoid psychedelia, the Rogers tune opens with backwards guitar and other sounds of the 1960s that could not be more cliché. Having avoided other psychedelic music (except for the opening to CCR's 'Run Through the Jungle' [1970]), the tune sounds even more psychedelic because of the omission of other psychedelic music. 'Stamping Ground' may sound like the classical music heard at Mr Lebowski's residence and during the landlord's dance piece, but knowing the composer Moondog was an eccentric blind man who chose to live on the streets of Manhattan for most of his life further illuminates the moment the Dude pieces everything together. Although not heard in the movie, in the full version of 'Stamping Ground' Moondog states in the middle piece: 'Machines were mice and men were lions once upon a time. But now that it's the opposite, it's twice upon a time.' These opposites are in the mixture of Moondog's worlds (classical and street) and paralleled in the Dude's moment of clarity. The topsy-turvy nature of Mr Lebowski's and the Dude's worlds is a result of their collision and, once recognized, the Dude reaches resolution by solving the mystery of the missing money.

But the final visit to Mr Lebowski is not the ultimate resolution. The Dude and Walter go bowling, but afterwards they are confronted by the Nihilists. After an altercation, Donny's heart attack and his cremation, the film resolves with a scene with the Dude and a last speech by the Stranger. During this final scene in the bowling alley, we hear Van Zandt's cover of the Rolling Stones's 'Dead Flowers', first in the bowling alley and then non-diegetically over the first part of the final credits. The lyrics to the song give a new message about the love of women:

Well, you're sitting back / In your rose pink Cadillac / Making bets on Kentucky Derby Day / I'll be in my basement room / With a needle and a spoon / And another girl can take my pain away.

Gone is the mystery of love and longing. The singer of the song obviously remembers his first love, as he 'won't forget to put roses on [her] grave', but he is over her and on to someone (and something) else who can take his pain away. This is a much less romantic view of love. And maybe the message is not one the Dude adheres to, as he does not choose the music and it is also heard non-diegetically. But as the penultimate piece of music in the movie, the contrast with other pieces on love and women cannot be ignored.

Finally, over the second half of the final credits Shawn Colvin's cover of 'Viva Las Vegas' can be heard, the tune slowed to a near ballad tempo. This creates a satirical edge to the tune, as if to say that the love of excess is over. Instead of 'long live Las Vegas', the message is more a remembrance and a farewell to such attitudes. Can we assume that from the experience that the Dude is wiser? All of the events of the movie are predicated on one moment of mistaken identity and urination on a rug. As a result, the Dude goes on an adventure, gets laid (but is then quickly dumped by his 'special lady friend'), loses his friend and bowling partner Donny, and his car and precious CCR tapes are destroyed. The movie is a bummer, man! But as the Dude replies to the Stranger when asked how it is going at the end of the movie: 'Ahh, you know. Strikes and gutters, ups and downs [...] The Dude abides.' And the music of *The Big Lebowski* clearly illustrates those ups and downs.

## Conclusion

Mapping the musical world surrounding the Dude, I understand the movie a bit better. I even 'hear' it better. Though most fans of the film gravitate to the images and sound bites in the film, understanding the music and its use (whether intended or coincidental) further illuminates the film.

One last observation on the music in *The Big Lebowski*. Most of the music and other cultural references in the movie can be sorted into four historical periods:

1. The time the Dude was a child or in high school and college (1946–62);
2. The Dude's life after dropping out of college (1966–72);
3. A period where he arguably would have hated the music of the time, including the Eagles (1972–78); and,
4. A period where some music from these earlier times was covered by other musicians (1990–95).

But it is the omission of anything from the 1980s that is an even more interesting observation. Except for the Dude's Walkman and his mentioning to Maude that he was a roadie for Metallica on the (fictional) 'Speed of Sound' tour, there is no mention or use of any music or other cultural icons from the 1980s! Given that the movie is set in 1990, the omission is relevant, as the time is the recent past of the movie. Furthermore, the musical covers made in the 1990s are all of songs from the 1960s and 1970s (The Chieftain's 'Hotel California' as part of the 40th anniversary of Elektra, ZZ Top's cover of 'Viva Las Vegas' that the fictional band 'Big Johnson''s version is based on, Van Zandt's take on the Stones's classic 'Dead Flowers' and Colvin's take on 'Viva Las Vegas' as part of a tribute to its songwriter Doc Pomus). I dare not read too much into this omission as only the Coen brothers or Burnett could explain the void and whether it was intentional or not. But I would not be a good cartographer if I were to ignore this tear or hole in the musical map of the Lebowski world. And not everything has to be tied together. ●

**Listening Deeply to *Lebowski*: One Fan's Attempt to Draw a Musical Map Surrounding the Dude**
Tom Zlabinger

**A MAP OF MUSIC in *THE BIG LEBOWSKI***

| Scene | Music the Dude chooses | Music the Dude does not choose | Non-diegetic music |
|---|---|---|---|
| Opening Tumble-weed Sequence | | | SONS OF THE PIONEERS: 'Tum-bling Tumble-weeds' |
| The Dude buys milk | | Muzak version of 'Tumbling Tumble-weeds' | |
| The Dude returns home | | | SONS OF THE PIONEERS: 'Tum-bling Tumble-weeds' |
| Opening Credits (and segue) | | | BOB DYLAN: 'The Man in Me' |
| The Dude explains what happened to his rug to Walter and Donny | | BOB DYLAN: 'The Man in Me' | |
| The Dude takes a rug and meets Bunny | | ESQUIVEL: 'Mucha Machacha' | |
| Walter pulls a gun on Smokey | | THE MONKS: 'I Hate You' | |
| The Dude listens to his messages | CAPTAIN BEEF-HART: 'Her Eyes are a Blue Million Miles' | | |
| Mr Lebowski tells the Dude of Bunny's abduction | | MOZART: Requiem | |
| Quintana Bowling Montage | | | THE CHIEFTAINS: 'Hotel California' |

| Scene | Music the Dude chooses | Music the Dude does not choose | Non-diegetic music |
| --- | --- | --- | --- |
| The Dude listens to his Walkman | Venice Beach League Playoffs | | |
| DREAM SE-QUENCE #1: The Dude flies after Maude (and segue) | | | BOB DYLAN: 'The Man in Me' |
| The Dude wakes up to no rug and beeping beeper | BOB DYLAN: 'The Man in Me' | | |
| The Dude picks up cellphone from Brandt | | KORNGOLD: Die tote Stadt/The Dead City | |
| The Dude and Walter drop off the ringer | CREEDENCE CLEARWATER REVIVAL: 'Run Through the Jungle' | | |
| The Dude does not answer ringing cellphone | | BOOKER T & THE M.G.'s: 'Behave Yourself' | |
| The Dude meets Maude | | | MEREDITH MONK: 'Walking Song' |
| Maude shows the Dude title credits of 'Logjammin'' | | PIERO PICCIONI: 'Traffic Boom' | |
| The Dude returns home from Maude's in a limo | | DEAN MARTIN: 'Standing on the Corner' | |
| The Dude explains to Walter about the toe at the diner | | DEBBIE REYN-OLDS: 'Tammy' | |

**Listening Deeply to *Lebowski*: One Fan's Attempt to Draw a Musical Map Surrounding the Dude**
Tom Zlabinger

| Scene | Music the Dude chooses | Music the Dude does not choose | Non-diegetic music |
|---|---|---|---|
| The Dude takes a bath | Song of the Whale: Ultimate Relaxation | | |
| The Dude explains to Walter and Donny about the Nihilists | | ELVIS COSTELLO: 'My Mood Swings' | |
| The Stranger talks to the Dude | | SONS OF THE PIONEERS: 'Tumbling Tumbleweeds' | |
| The Dude visits Maude | | THE RUSTAVI CHOIR: 'We Venerate Thy Cross' | |
| The Dude goes to the doctor | ELVIS COSTELLO: 'My Mood Swings' | | |
| The Dude drives home from the doctor | CREEDENCE CLEARWATER REVIVAL: 'Looking Out my Backdoor' | | |
| The Dude sees his landlord's dance piece | | MUSSORGSKY: Pictures at an Exhibition | |
| The Dude, Walter and Donny drive home after visiting Larry Sellers / The Dude props chair in front of door | SANTANA: 'Oye Como Va' | | |
| The beach party at Jackie Treehorn's | | | YMA SUMAC: 'Ataypura' |
| Inside Jackie Treehorn's home | | HENRY MANCINI: 'Lujon' | |

| Scene | Music the Dude chooses | Music the Dude does not choose | Non-diegetic music |
|---|---|---|---|
| Jackie Treehorn drugs the Dude | | TEO USUELLI: 'Piacere Sequence' | |
| DREAM SEQUENCE #2: 'Gutterballs' | | | KENNY ROGERS: 'Just Dropped In (To See What Condition My Condition Was In)' |
| The Dude sings in the cop car | Opening theme from Branded | | |
| The Dude gets thrown out of the cab | | EAGLES: 'Peaceful Easy Feeling' | |
| Bunny drives by in convertible | | BIG JOHNSON: 'Viva Las Vegas' | |

**Listening Deeply to *Lebowski*: One Fan's Attempt to Draw a Musical Map Surrounding the Dude**
Tom Zlabinger

## GO FURTHER

### Books

*The Big Lebowski: The Making of a Coen Brothers Film*
Tricia Cooke and William Preston Robertson (eds.)
(New York: W.W. Norton, 1998)

### Extracts/Essays/Articles

'Holding Out Hope for the Creedence: Music and the Search for the Real Thing in *The Big Lebowski*'
Diane Pecknold
In Edward P. Comentale and Aaron Jaffe (eds). *The Year's Work in Lebowski Studies* (Bloomington: Indiana University Press, 2009), pp. 276–94

'A Music Maker Happy to Be Just a Conduit'
Billy Altman
In *New York Times*, 24 February 2002, Available at: http://www.nytimes.com/2002/02/24/movies/music-a-music-maker-happy-to-be-just-a-conduit.html?src=pm

### Recordings

*The Big Lebowski: Original Motion Picture Soundtrack*, Various (Mercury, 1998)
*Volcano Songs*, Meredith Monk (ECM, 1997)

*Till the Night is Gone: A Tribute to Doc Pomus*, Various (Rhino, 1995)

*Greatest Hits*, ZZ Top (Warner Bros., 1992)

*Roadsongs*, Townes Van Zandt (Sugar Hill, 1993)

*Rubáiyát: Elektra's 40th Anniversary*, Various (Elektra, 1990)

*Die Mensch-Maschine/The Man-Machine*, Kraftwerk (EMI/Kling Klang, 1978)

*Hotel California*, Eagles (Asylum, 1976)

*Autobahn*, Kraftwerk (Philips/Vertigo, 1974)

*Eagles*, Eagles (Asylum, 1972)

*Clear Spot*, Captain Beefheart (Reprise, 1972)

*Sticky Fingers*, Rolling Stones (Rolling Stones, 1971)

*Abraxas*, Santana (Columbia, 1970)

*Cosmo's Factory*, Creedence Clearwater Revival (Fantasy, 1970)

*New Morning*, Bob Dylan (Columbia, 1970)

*Moondog*, Moondog (CBS, 1969)

*The First Edition*, Kenny Rogers and the First Edition (Reprise, 1967)

*Black Monk Time*, The Monks (Polydor, 1966)

*Latin-Esque*, Juan García Esquivel (RCA Victor, 1962)

*Green Onions*, Booker T. & the M.G.'s (Atlantic, 1962)

*Sings Duke Ellington*, Nina Simone (Colpix, 1962)

*Mr. Lucky Goes Latin*, Henry Mancini (RCA Victor, 1961)

'Tammy'/'French Heels', Debbie Reynolds (Coral, 1957)

'Standing on the Corner'/'Watching the World Go By', Dean Martin (Capitol, 1956)

*Voice of the Xtabay*, Yma Sumac (Capitol, 1950)

'Cowboy Camp Meetin''/'Tumbling Tumbleweeds', Sons of the Pioneers (RCA Victor, 1946)

**Websites**

*The Big Lebowski Wiki*, http://thebiglebowski.wikia.com

Chapter
10

# Abiding Sublimely: From Eastern Philosophies to *The Big Lebowski*

JZ Long

→ **May all beings be at ease ... May all beings be at ease!**
(Gautama Buddha)

**'Just take it easy, man ... Just take it easy.'**
(The Dude)

The amount of scholarly research dealing with the Coen brothers' *The Big Lebowski* is already legendary. While some scholars have analysed the film in terms of cinematic *genre* (from film noir to westerns to comedies to buddy movies) and *technique* (including 'cine-mimetic syntax' and 'spectatorial authorship'), others have used literary concepts like irony, myth, postmodernism and even literary critic Mikhail Bakhtin's idea of 'carnivalesque social critique', to interrogate the film's deeper meanings. Still others have examined the film from the perspectives of class, gender, sexuality and ethnicity, and there have even been academic papers written by students, from undergraduate theses to doctoral dissertations.

Recent analyses of *Lebowski* have sought to illustrate the film's philosophical importance. Three recent collections in particular – Mark Conrad's *The Philosophy of the Coen Brothers* (2008, updated edition 2012), Edward Comentale and Aaron Jaffe's *The Year's Work in Lebowski Studies* (2009), and Peter Fosl's *The Big Lebowski and Philosophy: Keeping Your Mind Limber with Abiding Wisdom* (2012) – exemplify this type of analysis. *The Philosophy of the Coen Brothers*, for example, used Søren Kierkegaard's existentialism to understand 'a man who wasn't there'; Friedrich Nietzsche's concept of nihilism to analyse, fittingly, *Lebowski*'s nihilists; and Immanuel Kant's moral imperative to interrogate moral codes in *No Country for Old Men* (2007). *The Year's Work in Lebowski Studies*, on the other hand, used Karl Marx's *Communist Manifesto*; Paul de Man's concept of 'hyperirony'; and Freudian psychoanalysis to explore bowling alleys, White Russians and 'metaphoric tumbleweeds', respectively. Fosl's collection, a volume in the popular Philosophy and Pop Culture Series published by Wiley-Blackwell, included articles dealing with Kurt Godel's mathematical logic, Epicurus's hedonism, Aristotle's virtue theory and Freud's Oedipal complex. Each of these books illustrates the philosophical depth of the film.

Another theme which emerged has been the arrival of works on linking the film to various systems of thought which can be referred to as spiritual philosophies. As defined in the *Encyclopedia of Religion* (2004), spirituality is 'the concern of human beings with their appropriate relationships to the cosmos'. (As an aside, this comprehensive text served as an invaluable reference for the background material discussed below.) Through a close examination of several texts – including *The Dude De Ching* (2010), *The Abide Guide: Living Like Lebowski* (2011) and *The Dude and the Zen Master* (2012) – this chapter illustrates how they build on the ideas of such prominent eastern figures as Laozi, Buddha and Lin Yutang to articulate a radical new spiritual philosophy as exemplified in the Dude, the film's protagonist. In these unsettled times, this philosophy provides us with the means for abiding, as Buddha suggests, sublimely.

## From Daoism to Dudeism

Laozi was a Chinese scholar who lived from 604–531 BCE and is most famous for writing the Dao-de-Jing. His ideas of *dao* and *de* are of particular importance. *Dao* is the

**Abiding Sublimely:**
**From Eastern Philosophies to *The Big Lebowski***
JZ Long

Chinese word for road, path or way, while *de* refers to virtue, goodness and generosity or 'the inherent force and power that moves the world'. Taken together (*dao-de*), the term is most often translated as 'morality'. This moral system, however, distinguishes itself from traditional theistic religions that explain the universe according to the designs of a divine creator. Often referred to as a humanist, or human – rather than god-centred – philosophy, Laozi maintains that salvation is therefore achieved by focusing on a path towards virtue. Emphasizing the impermanence of life rather than the futile attempts to control it, Laozi argues that the universe is governed by unconscious processes of ebb and flow, of creation and destruction, or what he famously calls *yin* and *yang*. More widely translated than any other book except the Christian Bible, the 81 brief theses in Laozi's Dao-de-Jing have come to serve as a spiritual guide for Daoists, and Dudeists, worldwide.

The founding father of Dudeism (aka The Church of the Latter-Day Dude), Oliver Benjamin (also known as the Rev. Oliver Benjamin as well as The Dudely Lama) came to a sudden realization while rewatching the film in Thailand in 2005. As cited by *The Way of the Dude*, Benjamin recalls that he

> suddenly felt as if I'd seen a story that put all the difficulties of modern life into a manageable perspective [...] a story about how to live your life, how to deal with conflict, and how to maintain peace of mind in a world that's gone crazy.

Seeking to share these insights, Benjamin sought out others who appreciated this spiritual revelation. What started out as a small group of fans grew into what Benjamin and his colleague Dwayne Eutsey now refer to as the Dudeist 'religion'.

In *The Dude De Ching*, the verses of the Dao-de-Jing are reinterpreted by The Church in order to illustrate its relevance for its Dudeist practitioners. In his introduction to *The Dude De Ching*, 'Arch Dudeship' Dwayne Eutsey notes that

> the *Tao Te Ching* is the perfect expression of Taoism's *wu wei* of life [...] a life of creative quietude in which [the mind] can flow with the Tao (or Way) of the universe [...] [and] Taoism's *wu wei* ethos of just taking it easy, man, and rolling with the cosmic flow.

As the church puts it, 'The Dude is the way'. According to Dudeist philosophy, 'man long endures ups and downs, strikes and gutters' in a complex and chaotic world, but the Dudeist is 'He who knows when to take it easy', especially when events are within our control. From the film's beginning to its end, the Dude is thrust into violent situations not of his own making and yet he continues to seek a path of serenity for both himself and others. As noted throughout *The Dude De Ching*, we must become 'calmer' in order to 'abide' like the Dude.

As The Dudely Lama writes in *The Dudespaper*,

> Dudeism is a belief system that teaches us that the universe wants us to take it easy [...] It's about finding ways to keep your heart light when the bastards are trying to get you down. It's basically Taoism meets *The Big Lebowski*, plus a bit scoop of humanism and perhaps a sprinkling of Buddhism.

In 'The Take It Easy Manifesto', the Arch Dudeship adds,

> From what is Buddhism trying to liberate us? *Suffering.* To what state of being is Buddhism trying to bring us? *Nirvana.* By what means does Buddhism attempt to do this? *The Noble Eightfold Path.* [...] Now let's apply it to Dudeism: From what is Dudeism trying to liberate us? *Thinking that's too uptight.* To what state of being is Dudeism trying to bring us? *Just taking it easy, man.* By what means does Dudeism attempt to do this? *Abiding.*

The manifesto goes on to describe both Dude- and un-Dude-like behaviours, the core experience of 'Abiding and takin'er [*sic*] easy', and an ethical system where, to quote the Stranger, 'sometimes you eat the bear, and well, sometimes the bear, he eats you'.

In order to spread the word, The Church also runs a website (*Dudeism.com: Your Answer for Everything*), publishes *The Dudespaper*, an online 'lifestyle magazine for the deeply casual', and has started the Abide University, a new 'institution of higher learning'. The Church has also published *The Abide Guide: Living Like Lebowski*, an engaging book which connects the Dude to other 'great dudes in history' (including Laozi, Buddha and Jesus), as well as linking Dudeism to such radical philosophies as feminism, Rastafarianism and transcendentalism. Divided into two large sections: Dudeist history and Dudeist practices, the book articulates, against the traditional 'uptight way', a 'Dude Way', which, in complete 'contrast to the uptight and superficial life that society often demands we live, [...] is really about living an authentic life that grows naturally from a laid-back sensibility'. Returning us full circle to the teachings of Laozi, the Church concludes that 'the Dude shows us a way to be "at home" in the world even without a destination in mind. Like an old Taoist monk, he goes with the flow even as he remains utterly still'.

### From Buddhism to Dudeism

Gautama Buddha was born around 563 BCE in Lumbini, Nepal. At the age of 29, he is said to have left his home to study under various Indian philosophers before embarking on a far-reaching quest to teach his new insights about his understanding of the nature of the universe. Gautama argued that, through disciplined thinking and ascetic practices, one could discover the truth (*dharma*) about this reality and therefore achieve enlightenment (*nirvana*). Through intense meditation and discipline, one could learn to see that the inherent suffering (*dukkha*) of the world was caused by an inability to understand the true nature of reality: emptiness (*sunyata*) and impermanence (*anitta*). Buddha summarized these views in the 'Four Noble Truths' and developed an 'Eight-Fold Noble Path' that, like Laozi, sets out that practitioners could work on their own enlightenment. One of the most well-known schools of Buddhist thought has been that of Zen Buddhism, a variant originating in mid-twelfth century Japan. While the Sotoshu school of Japanese Zen stressed the practice of *zazen* ('sitting zen'), the competing Rinzaishu school developed the use of *koans*, or short parables, to evoke sudden enlightenment on the part of the student.

Bernie Glassman, a practising Zen Buddhist for over fifty years, has recently focused his attention on Zen concepts found in *The Big Lebowski* through his publication of *The Dude and the Zen Master*, a bestselling collaboration with the Dude himself, Jeff Bridges. Transcribing a weekend of conversation, the book touches on topics ranging from Bridgess' acting and personal lives to the deeper meaning of the Dude's answering machine message ('The Dude is not in'). As Bridges writes in the book's introduction, 'Bernie has been interested for some time now in making Zen more accessible in our times and culture, relevant and down-to-earth, and he felt that *Lebowski* did that big-time'.

Roshi Glassman (Roshi is a term for 'old teacher', itself a translation of the word Laozi!) is also the founder of the Zen Peacemakers, an international organization committed to a 'socially engaged' form of Buddhism dedicated to 'clos[ing] the gap between what society is and what it could be'. As part of this work, Glassman has developed a number of *koans* and precepts connecting the ethics of *The Big Lebowski* to his Zen practices. Many concepts are at work here, including those of 'not-knowing', tying things together, strikes and gutters, and compassion, giving and receiving. In the 'Lebowski Precepts', on the other hand, Glassman compares Buddha's 'three refuges' and 'pure precepts' with his own 'three tenets' in order to articulate the Dude's 'three what-have-you's': The Dude is Not In, The Dude Abides and Enjoyin' My Coffee. As with Buddha's transition from his noble truths to his eight-fold path, the Peacemakers build on the 'three what-have-you's' by developing ten 'grave precepts' to avoid, including not discussing others' faults, not blaming others and not being stingy.

These themes are also developed throughout *I'm a Lebowski, You're a Lebowski* (2007), a book by the founders of the Lebowski Fest which also offers a Dudeist path, or, as they put it, 'the Duddha's (or El Duddharino's) way'. According to the authors, for example, Buddha's right mindfulness becomes the Duddha's 'The Dude minds', right speech becomes 'I'll tell you what I'm blathering about', and right effort is translated as 'Just take it easy, man'. And in *Wired* Magazine, Matthew Hutson adds to this discussion between Buddhism and Dudeism, citing such 'teachings' as not getting hung up on labels, rolling with the punches and appreciating the connectedness of all things. These sample treatises easily illustrate how Buddhist concepts inform Dudeist philosophy, mutually strengthening each other in the process. Between the world's ten million Zen practitioners and Dudeism's 180,000 certified 'priests', there are a multitude of avenues for continued spiritual development.

### From Lin Yutang to the Dude

In two thought-provoking essays on his *Reality Sandwich* blog, Argentine-born novelist and blogger Guido Mina di Sospiro references a number of spiritual philosophies in order to understand the Dude's unique way of life. Focusing on the Dude's pacifist attitude, Sospiro marvels at the Dude's calmness amidst the 'circus full of hostile lunatics who want something from him and will insult him, threaten him and beat him to get it'. As Sospiro notes, however,

> nothing seems to phase [*sic*] the Dude. Yes, he gets angry (to the point that Walter tells him: "Come on. You're being very un-Dude."), swears constantly, and talks back at Walter and many other unreasonable people [...] but soon he will be stirring himself another White Russian, or will have a smoke, or relax in a warm bath [...] Like a mystic, he focuses on the big picture. Better yet, like a true mystic, he doesn't focus at all.

Citing Laozi, Sospiro writes that there 'is something transcendental about this: the Dude rises above all circumstances'. After all, Sospiro adds 'the Dude abides', remaining 'level-headed, tolerant, and consistently non-violent' and even making 'allowances for a lot of overaggressive people, out there, who will act like very hostile lunatics'. Sospiro argues that his refusal to 'become bitter, or angry, or revengeful' is evidence that the Dude 'doesn't do, he is'. As Sospiro notes,

> Even when provoked, he harms no one. He cares little about money and is, in essence, a sensible, honest man with the kind of patience and tolerance that belongs to the spiritually gifted. He doesn't preach; now in the wisdom of his maturity, he never would; he just abides.'

Such a spiritual ethos, to use the parlance of our times, leads Sospiro to suggest that, 'With more people like him, the world would improve markedly'.

In his second essay, Sospiro uses ideas from Chinese philosopher and activist Lin Yutang. Like Laozi and Buddha before him, Yutang is critical of those world-views which posit an afterlife, arguing that such a focus prevents us from dealing with the sensual and embodied nature of reality. As Sospiro puts it, 'being alive, living, matters' immensely for Yutang. His book *The Importance of Living* (1937), for example, states that a 'philosophy, which is the exercise of the spirit *par excellance*', needs to deal with reality as it exists in the here-and-now rather than at some future place or time. Yutang even questions life itself, arguing that positing a meaning to life 'begs the question' of life *having* a purpose. According to Yutang, 'Had there been a purpose of design in life, it should have not been so puzzling and vague and difficult to find out.' Yutang concludes, therefore, that only by developing a more materialistic philosophy - a 'new humanism' which emphasizes the material world of bodies and things - can we understand the world as well as our roles and pleasures within it. In chapters on 'The Feast of Life', 'The Importance of Loafing' and 'The Enjoyment of Living', for example, Yutang emphasizes such things as the importance of good food, idleness and lying in bed. Such Dude-like sentiments echo other ideas discussed by Yutang, including intuitive thinking and non-conformism.

Incorporating these insights, Sospiro argues that while the Dude's life as seen in the film is one of constant stress and violence, the Dude does experience 'brief interludes' of peace in which his engagement in such 'sensual pleasures' as smoking, drinking, bathing and practicing t'ai chi all 'add to his spiritual enjoyment of life'. Illuminating how these types of sensual and spiritual practices interact, Sospiro notes that at the end of the film the Dude is nevertheless 'shown smiling [...] and, in essence, abiding [...] He does a terrific job in remaining balanced, level-headed and reasonable; he does abide, and how'. Thus, to the profound question of 'How should one live one's life?', scholar Mark Cyzyk argues that Yutang's preference is for the 'amiable loafer who wanders through life, learning, loving, living. He is a good-natured Renaissance Man, dabbling here and there [...] earthbound, a man of biology and of his senses [...] And most of all, he's eminently "reasonable."' Cyzyk adds that this philosophy echoes those of Marcus Aurelius, Henry David Thoreau and Ralph Waldo Emerson, who, like Yutang, 'illustrates a life, and how to live one'. To this list we can add the Dude, who perfectly embodies the Renaissance Man's amiability, reasonableness and good nature.

## Conclusion

Lest one think that these ideas remain theoretical, the philosophical themes of *The Big Lebowski* are profoundly impacting real people in their everyday lives. In a time of global upheaval and impending ecological, moral and physical disasters, the Dude serves for many individuals as a guide for how to model one's life in the face of such overwhelming suffering. As one fan points out, the Dude

> has a really simple life. And something for him that tied it all together was taken and he is trying to get it back. He's not really sure how he's doing it and all these forces are acting for him or against him. He just goes along trusting that it will work out.

Another fan and Lebowski Fest organizer adds that 'Everyone can understand the Dude. You know, sometimes you just got to let go, just like the Dude. The Dude abides'. Others argue that the Dude is a 'carefree relaxed person, who speaks his mind and does what he likes to', a 'Zen master' who 'takes things as they come' and 'doesn't accept society's version of what life is supposed to be'. One of the best sources of these ideas comes from the *Dudeism* website, where the publishers offered a free copy of their book to those who e-mailed them about why they love the film. With over a thousand responses, people wrote that the film 'really ties my life together', serving as 'a philosophy for life', 'a metaphor for anti-existential anti-angst' and 'a great lesson about life, friendship, confrontation, death and the meaning of the great design of being alive'. For many, *The Big Lebowski* is not just a film but 'a way of life' that 'expresses the way everyone should live'.

This brings us back to the two quotes at the beginning of the chapter. The first quote is from the Buddha's last sermon, where he reminds his followers of the way to achieve true enlightenment. He states, among other things, that Buddhist practitioners should be, among other things, 'straightforward and gentle in speech', 'peaceful and calm, and wise and skillful', 'not holding to fixed views' and 'not proud and demanding in nature'. In a passage that encapsulates the Dude's own ethos, the Buddha notes that one should be 'humble and not conceited, contented and easily satisfied, unburdened with duties and frugal in their ways'. Only in this way, he states, may we all be 'at ease' and achieve a state of 'sublime abiding'. While we have a long road of suffering ahead, it is, as one Dudeist writes, 'through the way of the Dude' that we can learn 'how to live life to the fullest, how to obtain true happiness'. Taking it easy in a violent world that seeks to beat him down, the Dude, like us, can still abide. ●

## GO FURTHER

### Books

*The Big Lebowski and Philosophy: Keeping Your Mind Limber with Abiding Wisdom*
Peter S. Fosl (ed.)
(Hoboken: Wiley, 2012)

*The Dude and the Zen Master*
Jeff Bridges and Bernie Glassman
(New York: Blue Rider Press, 2012)

*The Philosophy of the Coen Brothers*
Mark T. Conrad (ed.)
(Lexington: University Press of Kentucky, 2012)

**Abiding Sublimely:**
**From Eastern Philosophies to *The Big Lebowski***
JZ Long

*The Abide Guide: Living Like Lebowski*
Oliver Benjamin and Dwayne Eutsey
(Berkeley: Ulysses, 2011)

*The Dude De Ching: A Dudeist Interpretation of the Tao Te Ching*
The Church of the Latter-Day Dude
(Scotts Valley, CA: CreateSpace, 2010)

*The Year's Work in Lebowski Studies*
Edward P. Comentale and Aaron Jaffe (eds)
(Bloomington: Indiana University Press, 2009)

*I'm a Lebowski, You're a Lebowski: Life, The Big Lebowski, and What Have You*
Bill Green, Ben Peskoe, Will Russell and Scott Shuffitt
(New York: Bloomsbury, 2007)

*Encyclopedia of Religion*
Lindsay Jones (ed.)
(Farmington Hills: Thomson Gale, 2004; 2nd edn)

*The Importance of Living*
Lin Yutang
(New York: Reynal & Hitchcock, 1937)

**Essays/Extracts/Articles**

'Zen and the art of being the Dude'
Matthew Hutson
*Wired.* November 2012, p. 116.

'*The Importance of Living* by Lin Yutang'
Mark Cyzyk
*Philosophy Now.* No. 71 (2009), pp. 39–40.

**Online**

'The importance of living: Lin Yutang meets the Dude – An esoteric take on *The Big Lebowski*, pt. 2'
Guido Mina di Sospiro
*Reality Sandwich.* 8 January 2013,

http://www.realitysandwich.com/lin_yutang_meets_big_lebowski_pt_2.
'An esoteric take on *The Big Lebowski*'
Guido Mina di Sospiro
*Reality Sandwich*. 4 December 2012,
http://www.realitysandwich.com/esoteric_take_big_lebowski.

'Is *The Big Lebowski* a cultural milestone?'
Finlo Rohrer
*BBC News*. 10 October 2008,
http://news.bbc.co.uk/2/hi/uk_news/magazine/7662943.stm.

'Bowling, "The Dude" and 200 "Achievers": Showing of cult film "The Big Lebowski" draws the faithful'
Wyatt Benjamin
*San Francisco Chronicle*. 27 September 2004,
sfgate.com/bayarea/article/Bowling-The-Dude-and-200-Achievers-Showing-2691262.php.

Dudeism.com: Your Answer for Everything, www.dudeism.com

The Dudespaper: A Lifestyle Magazine for the Deeply Casual, www.dudespaper.com

The Way of the Dude: A Documentary in the Making, thewayofthedude.com

Zen Peacemakers, zenpeacemakers.org

# Contributor Details

## EDITOR

**Zachary Ingle** is a Ph.D. candidate in Film and Media Studies at the University of Kansas. A graduate of Howard Payne University, Baylor University and North Carolina A&T State University, he previously edited *Robert Rodriguez: Interviews* (University Press of Mississippi, 2012), and co-edited *Gender and Genre in Sports Documentaries* and *Identity and Myth in Sports Documentaries* (both Scarecrow Press, 2013) with David Sutera. He has contributed to a dozen film books for Intellect (including writing chapters for the Fan Phenomena volumes on *Star Wars* and Marilyn Monroe), and his articles and reviews have appeared in *Literature/Film Quarterly*, *Journal of American Culture*, *Journal of Sport History*, *Mass Communication and Society*, *Film & History* and *Film-Philosophy*, among others.

## CONTRIBUTORS

**Sheri Chinen Biesen** is Associate Professor of Film History at Rowan University and author of *Blackout: World War II and the Origins of Film Noir* (Johns Hopkins University Press, 2005). She received her Ph.D. at University of Texas at Austin, MA and BA at University of Southern California School of Cinema and has taught film at USC, University of California, University of Texas and England. She has contributed to *Film and History*, *Historical Journal of Film, Radio and Television*, *Quarterly Review of Film and Video*, *Literature/Film Quarterly*, *Film Noir: The Encyclopedia*, *Film Noir Reader 4*, *Gangster Film Reader*, *Film Noir: The Directors*, *Popular Culture Review*, *The Historian*, *Television and Television History*, *American Jewish History* and edited *The Velvet Light Trap*. Her next book on film noir is due out soon.

**Randall Clark** is Associate Professor of Communication and Media Studies at Clayton State University in Morrow, Georgia. He teaches classes in film history and film genre. His publications include the book, *At a Theater or Drive-In Near You: The History, Politics and Culture of the American Exploitation Film* (Garland, 1995), in addition to articles on the films of Pam Grier, the MGM musical *The Glass Slipper*, George Cukor's *Justine*, the American television series *Perry Mason* and *Voyage to the Bottom of the Sea*, and the children's book series *Freddy the Pig*, among others. He is pleased to have eaten lunch one Saturday afternoon at Lebowski's Neighborhood Grill in Charlotte, North Carolina.

**Keith Clavin** is completing a dissertation in Victorian literature at Auburn University. His research interests include the history of economics, western philosophy and comedy. He has written articles about Thomas Hardy and Charles Dickens and hopes to continue studying contemporary film and television.

**Jeremy Hehl** is a film-maker and entrepreneur in the Kansas City area. He graduated from the University of Kansas with dual BA degrees in film and American history. He and his wife live in Lawrence, Kansas. His company BTH Media Group makes around two artistic films a year, and conducts business in the Kansas City Metro area. His goals are to eventually finish a Ph.D., and to one day go to the Oscars. He enjoys films of all types, social gatherings with friends and colleagues, and also writing in his spare time. He's been told on more than one occasion that he's the laziest man in Douglas County, Kansas.

**Andrew Howe** is Associate Professor of History at La Sierra University, where he teaches courses in film history and theory, popular culture, and American history. Recent publications include articles on the evolution of the hot dog as bellwether of late-nineteenth-century immigration, criticisms of manifest destiny in *Avatar* and race and racism in *Star Wars*. Current research projects involve the rhetoric of fear employed during the recent invasion of the Everglades by Burmese Pythons, as well as the debate over the supposed rediscovery of the Ivory-billed Woodpecker in Arkansas. These two works are conceived of as chapters in a book-length project exploring the manner in which societies translate environmental events by employing the familiar rhetorical strategies and vocabularies of existing, sociological problems.

**Jeff Jaeckle** is the editor of *Film Dialogue* (Wallflower, 2013). His writings on cinema have also appeared in *Film Quarterly*, *New Review of Film and Television Studies*, *Quarterly Review of Film and Video* and the *Oxford Handbook of American Literary Naturalism*. He holds a doctorate from the University of Texas at Austin and currently teaches at Portland Community College.

**Peter C. Kunze** is Lecturer in the Writing and Critical Inquiry Program at the University at Albany, SUNY. He completed his Ph.D. in twentieth-century American literature and film at Florida State University, where his research and teaching interests included comedy, masculinity and children's culture. Currently, he is editing a contributed volume on Wes Anderson and working on a study of sincerity in recent film and literature.

**JZ Long** is Assistant Professor of Communications at Wilson College in Chambersburg, Pennsylvania and holds interdisciplinary degrees in political and cultural economy, popular culture, and cultural studies. He has taught at the collegiate level for over fifteen years, including courses in interpersonal and group communications, cultural theory and digital design. Recent publications include analyses of the Hummer automobile, comic-book fanzines and popular cinema. He has also served as an ordained priest in The Church of the Latter-Day Dude since 2007.

**Paul Rogalus** teaches English at Plymouth State University. His full-length play *Crawling From the Wreckage* was produced in New York City in February 2002 by the American Theatre of Actors, and his one-act plays have been produced in New York, Chicago and Boston. His short screenplay, 'Sid and Walt', won screenwriting contests at the Wildsound Film Festival in Toronto and at the PictureStart Film Festival in New York City last year. A chapbook of his micro-stories entitled *Meat Sculptures* was published by Green Bean Press in 2001.

**Tom Zlabinger** is Assistant Professor of Music at York College/CUNY in New York City and is the director of the York College Big Band and the York College Blue Notes & Summer Jazz Program. He is a professional bass player and an ethnomusicologist, holding a BA from Grinnell College, an MA from Queens College/CUNY, and a Ph.D. from the Graduate Center/CUNY. His dissertation is entitled 'Free from Jazz: Jazz and Improvised Music Scene in Vienna after Ossiach (1971–2011)'. His current research interests include conducting, improvisation and its pedagogy, and music in film and video games.

# Image Credits

**From *The Big Lebowski* (the film)**

Chapter 1: Figs. 1-3 page 10
Chapter 3: Fig. 1 page 33
Chapter 5: Figs. 1-4 page 49, 51-52, 54

**Additional Images**

Chapter 2: Fig. 1 page 21 http://www.sporcle.com
Fig. 2 page 23 http://www.facebook.com
Fig. 3 page 24 http://dudespaper.com
Chapter 3: Fig. 2 page 34 Courtesy of Joe Poletta
Source - http://www.flickr.com/photos/vidmon/6053850132/
Author - Joe Poletta (user "vidmon" on Flickr)
Fig. 3 page 35 http://lebowskifest.com
Fig. 4 page 36 http://lebowskifest.com
Fig. 5 page 37 http://lebowskifest.com
Chapter 4: Figs. 1-2 page 42 http://www.cafepress.com
Figs. 3-5 page 43 http:www.ebay.com
Fig. 6 page 44 http://www.themovieshop.com
Figs. 7-8 page 44 http://www.ebay.com
Fig. 9 page 45 http://www.fantasytoyland.com
Fig. 10 page 46 http://dudeism.com
Chapter 6: Fig. 1 page 66 http://www.runleiarun.com/lebowski
Fig. 2 page 67 Courtesy of Steph Cathro
Fig. 3 page 68 Courtesy of Wojciech Wilczak
Fig. 4 page 68 Courtesy of Daniel Phai
Fig. 5 page 69 Courtesy of Steph Cathro
Chapter 8: Figs. 1-2 pages 84-85 http://www.youtube.com
Fig. 3 page 86 http://www.facebook.com
Fan Appreciation no. 1 page 26 Courtesy of Frankie Steele
Fan Appreciation no. 2 page 58 Courtesy of Adam Bertocci
Fan Appreciation no. 3 page 90 Courtesy of Kim Barber

# 'SOMETIMES, THERE'S A MAN, WELL, HE'S THE MAN FOR HIS TIME AND PLACE. HE FITS RIGHT IN THERE. AND THAT'S THE DUDE, IN LOS ANGELES.'

**THE STRANGER**

www.ingramcontent.com/pod-product-compliance
Lightning Source LLC
LaVergne TN
LVHW060728310826
846742LV00016B/57